Tasting
the Past

Tasting the Past

Recipes from Antiquity

JACQUI WOOD

Cover Illustration: Utro_na_more/iStockphoto

First published 2009, as part of *Tasting the Past: Recipes from the Stone Age to the Present*, and 2001, as part of *Prehistoric Cooking*

This edition published 2020

The History Press
97 St George's Place, Cheltenham,
Gloucestershire, GL50 3QB
www.thehistorypress.co.uk

British Library Cataloguing in Publication Data.
A catalogue record for this book is available from the British Library.

ISBN 978 0 7509 9225 1

Typesetting and origination by The History Press
Printed and bound in Great Britain by TJ International Ltd.

Contents

Introduction

BRITISH FOOD HAS been hard to categorise in the past compared to the very distinctive cuisines of countries such as Italy, France and Germany. This is because it is an amalgamation of all of them, in the same way that the English language is a combination of five European languages: Celtic, Latin, Saxon, Viking and Norman. Our cuisine, too, is a combination of the typical foods of those that once conquered Britain over a thousand years ago.

But Britain's assimilation of the foods of other cultures did not stop after the Norman Conquest. During the medieval period, the spices brought from the Crusades by the Normans were used in almost every dish by those who could afford them. When Britain itself began to have colonies, the culinary embellishments to our diet began again. During the Elizabethan period, strange produce coming from the New World was adopted with relish by our forebears.

The Civil War period introduced Puritan restrictions to our daily fare, making it against the law to eat a mince pie on Christmas Day because it was thought a decadent Papist tradition. The Georgians took on chocolate and coffee with gusto and even moulded their business transactions around the partaking of such beverages. But it was really not until the Victorian period – when it was said that the sun never set on the British Empire – that our diet became truly global in nature.

This book will hopefully become a manual for those readers who want to put on a themed dinner party, providing a wide selection of recipes from each period in history. I have not included those recipes that I feel you would never want to make, but instead have focused on dishes that will allow you to experience what it was really like to eat during those particular periods. No one, apart from the truly adventurous among you, is going to acquire a cow's udder from the butcher and stuff it as they did in the medieval period, or stuff a fish's stomach with chopped cod's liver!

Each chapter will begin with a brief introduction to the foods of the period that I found particularly fascinating during my research, and will end with the traditional festive food of the period. If you want to celebrate your Christmas in a completely different way, why not try a pagan Celtic spread or a Roman feast?

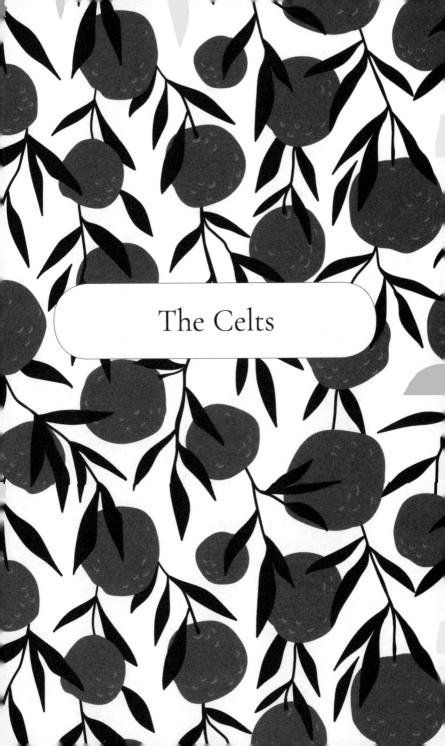

The Celts

IF I HAD to sum up one item of food that really says 'Celtic', it would have to be bacon or ham. The first Celtic society in Europe came from the Hallstatt region of Austria, where the famous salt mines are today. These people were in fact salt miners, and when archaeologists came across their remains in the labyrinth of tunnels in the Hallstatt mountains, they were well preserved due to the salt surrounding them. The Romans even commented on the fine quality of their salt pork and salt lamb, which were sold at the time in the markets as far south as Rome. So if you want to make yourself a quick and tasty authentic Celtic breakfast, make yourself a bacon sandwich with butter on brown bread and you are eating a bit of Celtic history!

On the whole, Celtic food was simple and unadulterated, with lots of meat, fish, bread and butter and chunks of cheese. Their main vegetable crops were beans and peas, and the rest of their vegetables they still gathered from the surrounding countryside and seashore. Vegetables were primarily leaves and stems, as the root vegetables we know today only arrived in Britain at the time of the Roman Conquest.

I devised the recipes below from a variety of sources from the archaeological record. Until I wrote my book *Prehistoric Cooking*, no one had attempted to try and discover what recipes our prehistoric forbears might have used. There was a school of thought arguing that, unless you found the actual residue of a particular meal in a pot, then you could not say categorically that our ancestors ate it. I, however, approached the subject in a different way. If we watch a TV documentary about an Amazonian tribe, we all assume that if there were tasty plants near them in the forest they would have known about them and eaten them. So I did not see why our ancestors should have been any different. I started to look at the pollen record around prehistoric settlements and, if the plants were tasty, then I put them in my recipes. I also looked at some lesser-known cooking techniques such as clay baking and water pit cooking.

There are also some lesser-known quotes by classical historians about the Celtic diet that add to this picture. One might assume that if you are going back as far as the Celtic period, something as basic as bread might be a bit hard and chewy, but this was not the case, as a quotation from the Roman historian Pliny illustrates:

When the corn of Gaul and Spain of the kinds we have stated is steeped to make beer the foam that forms on the surface in the process is for leaven, in consequence of which those races have a lighter kind of bread than others.

He is clearly talking about yeasted bread, which we tend to think was not eaten until much later. On the whole, the Celtic diet was varied, healthy and very tasty. One year I was doing a lot of cookery demonstrations and I found it impossible to weed my vegetable patch, as the weeds that grew around my vegetables were more valuable to me for cooking than the vegetables themselves! Here is a selection of recipes for you to try.

Lamb Boiled with Green Grass

This is the way people in prehistoric times cooked their meat in water pits. They covered the joint of meat, in this case a leg of lamb, in fresh green grass and tied it with string. Then they put it into a water pit and added hot stones to simmer for an hour or two until it was cooked. The grass not only protected the meat from the ash and stone grit in the trough, but also added flavour to it. Once cooked, the meat was taken out of its grass wrapping and crisped by the fire. This can be done in a modern kitchen by wrapping a leg of lamb in green grass and boiling it in a pot on the stove. When it is cooked, take it out of the grass and crisp it in the oven. You will never taste more delicious lamb than one that is cooked in this way. The grass seems to bring out its real flavour.

Dried Peas with Mint and Cream

225 g whole dried peas
25 g butter
A large bunch of chives
2 sprigs of mint
½ cup of cream
Salt to taste

Method

1. Soak the peas overnight in cold water.
2. Drain and cover with water and simmer until they are soft.
3. Drain the peas then put in a dish by the fire to keep warm.
4. Melt the butter in a pan and fry the chopped chives for a minute.
5. Add this to the cooked peas with the chopped mint and cream.
6. Season to taste.

Although quite simple, this is a delicious accompaniment to roast meat.

Leftover Pea Fritters

If any of the prior pea mixture is left over, it can be made into a nutritious fritter.

1. Add an egg to the peas and enough flour to bind it.
2. Shape into small cakes and roll into a mixture of finely chopped hazelnuts and flour.
3. Brown these cakes on a hot griddle.

These pea and nut fritters can be eaten hot or cold and are very good taken on long walks for a savoury snack.

Pease Pudding

This is a very traditional way to cook dried peas and can be well-suited to cooking in a water pit. Soak peas in water overnight and drain. Cook in fresh water with a few sprigs of thyme. Fry some sorrel (*Rumes Acetosella*) and chives, or any combination of wild vegetables, in some butter until soft. Mix with the cooked pea mixture and add an egg to bind, then put the mixture in a cloth that has been greased with butter and floured. Tie the cloth together tightly and drop into a water pit with the cooking meat. It will then absorb some of the meat stock from the pit-cooking process. Alternatively, it can be steamed: Try putting a simple wicker tray over a pot or cauldron of water. Put the pudding on top of this, place a large ceramic bowl over the pudding and set over a fire. This is a very simple and effective steamer that could also be used to cook fish.

Peas and Apple

Follow the prior recipe but instead of sorrel and chives fried in butter, use chives and chopped crab or cooking apples. This is an unusual combination but I think it's very tasty.

Beans and Carraway

These are like the modern broad bean (*Vicia faba*) but smaller and with a much thicker outer skin. In Britain these beans are called the 'tic bean' or 'British field bean' and, due to the thick skin, are now mainly cultivated for animal feed. This type of bean has been found throughout Iron Age Europe from Biskupin in Poland to Britain — hence the name 'Celtic Bean'. This bean needs overnight soaking and then boiling in fresh unsalted water for at least three hours. It then has to be processed to destroy the thick outer skin. I find the best way to do this is to grind them between two stones, as one might grind grain. Use a food processor if you do not have the time or inclination to be totally authentic. Borlotti beans are the closest modern equivalent found in stores.

This is my favourite way to eat Celtic beans.

1 kg cooked processed beans
or Borlotti beans

25 g butter

A big bunch of sorrel

A big bunch of chives

1 ramson bulb (*Allium ursinum*)
or two cloves of garlic

1 dessert spoon of caraway
seeds

Method

1. Fry the chopped sorrel, chives and ramson in the butter until soft.
2. Add the caraway seeds and the processed or Borlotti beans and salt.
3. Mix well and add a cup of water.
4. Cook gently over the fire until the water is absorbed.

Bean and Bacon Stew

250 g fatty bacon

2 sticks of celery

A bowl of pignuts (or use chopped parsnips)

2 leeks

250 g mushrooms

2 tsp mustard seeds

A sprig of thyme

500 g Borlotti beans

Method

1. Fry the chopped bacon until crisp and the fat comes out.
2. Chop and fry the celery, leeks and pignuts/parsnip until soft.
3. Add the chopped mushrooms, mustard seeds and thyme and stir well.
4. Add the Borlotti beans, two cups of water and a spoonful of salt.
5. Cook slowly for 1 hour until all the flavours have combined.
6. Serve with chunks of rye bread and butter.

Savoury Bean Fritters

These are made with the tinned Borlotti beans that you can find in any super market today; they are the nearest easily available alternative to the British field bean that the Celts used to grow. The skins are tough, though, so once drained, mash them with a fork before using. This is a great high-protein portable food, a savoury snack for those long winter walks and children love them.

125 g butter

A bunch of sorrel

125 g chopped hazelnuts

A bunch of sea beet (*Beta vularis*) or fat hen (*Chenopodium album*) – spinach will do if you can't get these.

1 tbsp grated horseradish

500 g Borlotti beans
(mashed with a fork)

1 egg

Salt to taste

Flour to mix

Method

1. Fry the sorrel in butter with the hazelnuts and sea beet, then add the grated horseradish and the beans.
2. Add the egg and salt and enough flour to make a stiff mixture.
3. Shape into rissoles and fry in more butter until brown. These are good hot or cold.

Lentils and Fat Hen or Sea Beet

125 g lentils	
2 leeks	
A good bunch of fat hen or sea beet leaves	
25 g butter	
1 tsp mustard seeds	
1 litre water	
3 tsbp wine vinegar	
Salt to taste	

Method

1. Wash the lentils, soak them for a few hours and drain.
2. Chop the leeks and fat hen and fry it in the butter with the mustard seeds.
3. Add the lentils and water and simmer until cooked.
4. Season to taste and stir in the vinegar.

Lentil and Mushroom Soup

125 g lentils

3 whole ramson plants or
2 cloves of garlic and a leek

25 g butter

A bowl of chopped
mushrooms

850 ml water

Salt to taste

1 tsp poppy seeds

Method

1. Soak and drain the lentils as before.
2. Chop the ramsons and fry in the butter.
3. Add the mushrooms and fry for another few minutes.
4. Add the water and the lentils and simmer for an hour.
5. Season with salt and add the poppy seeds.
6. Serve with large pieces of wholemeal bread.

Meat, Fish and Vegetable Stews

The convenience of cooking a meal in one pot must have been as obvious to our prehistoric ancestors as it is today. The recipes that follow are not the kind of meal that would have been made on a hunting expedition, but rather the sort that could have been made in a settlement. They may have been made with scraps of meat after butchering an animal, or they may have been used to cook tough meat that needed a longer cooking time. The archaeological evidence for meat-eating is strong — witness the large quantities of bone remains found in prehistoric rubbish dumps. In addition, the comments made by most classical historians about the Celts indicate that meat was the staple of their diet. Athenaeus says, 'Their food consists of a few loaves of bread, but large quantities of meat.' Still, it is quite possible that some did not eat meat and it is interesting to consider an alternative diet for them. To accommodate the increasing prevalence of vegetarians in our society, I have provided a meatless alternative to the first recipe, which serves event-sized portions.

Lamb Stew
(For a Large Party of Forty-five People)

I have made this stew many times for large public events and it always goes down very well. It can be adapted to suit vegetarian diets, too, by missing out the meat and frying a large quantity of chopped hazelnuts with the leeks in the butter.

1½ kg chopped or minced lamb
1 kg leeks – as an alternative to the wild onion
Ramsons
A good bunch of sorrel
A bunch of chickweed
2 bunches of chives
3 kg peas

2 large sprigs of mint

4 tsp salt

2 kg bulgar wheat (this is
chopped, pre-cooked and
dried wheat)

Method

1. Fry the lamb in a large pan until browned – there should be enough fat in the lamb without having to add any more.
2. Add the chopped sorrel, chives, leeks and chickweed and cook until tender.
3. Add the peas, mint, salt and enough water to cover it.
4. Simmer for approximately 30 minutes.
5. Add the bulgar wheat and simmer until all the stock has been absorbed.
6. Serve preferably in wooden bowls and eat at once.

Vegetable Stew (For Fifteen People)

125 g chopped hazelnuts

100 g butter

A bunch of sorrel

A bunch of chives and wild marjoram

1 kg chopped leeks

1 kg peas

1 sprig of mint

750 g bulgar wheat

2 tsp salt

Method

1. Fry the chopped nuts in the butter for 5 minutes.
2. Add the chopped leeks and herbs, except the mint, and cook until soft.
3. Add the peas, mint and salt and cover with water.
4. Simmer for 30 minutes.
5. Add the bulgar wheat and cook until all the stock is absorbed.
6. Serve at once.

This is a very tasty stew and could have been made in the springtime to use up the hazelnuts from the winter store.

Mutton Stew

1 loin of mutton cut into pieces (or lamb if not available)

2 tbsp stone-ground flour

28 g butter

2 tsp salt

28 g mustard seeds

Water

Method

1. Dust the mutton with the flour and salt and fry in the butter until brown.
2. Add the mustard seed and cover with water.
3. This can be cooked in an earthenware casserole dish with a lid. Mix a little flour and water in a bowl and use it to glue the lid to the dish – this makes an airtight seal. If you have an old pot it is better if, once sealed, it is placed at the edge of an open fire. Alternatively, it can be cooked in an oven for 3 hours.

There is nothing quite so tasty as eating a bowl of mutton stew with large chunks of bread out in the open. I would recommend it to those who are tired of conventional barbecue evenings.

Rich Mutton Stew with Juniper Berries

1 kg chopped mutton	
A piece of butter for frying	
4 whole ramson plants, leaves and bulbs (or use onion)	
1 litre dry red wine	
10 juniper berries	
1 tsp salt	
A piece of butter for frying	

Method

1. Fry the meat in a very hot pan with the butter.
2. Add the chopped onion or ramsons then add the red wine, juniper berries and salt.
3. Put into a pot and seal with a flour paste and lid.
4. Place in an oven or by a fire for at least 4 hours. The rich aroma of this dish is wonderful. Serve in bowls with chunks of bread to soak up the gravy.

Pigeon Stew

2 prepared pigeons

28 g lard

A sprig of marjoram and myrtle

A bunch of chives

A handful of sorrel

1 tsp salt

1 pint of blackberry wine (or dry red wine)

1 pint water

Method

1. Fry the pigeons (cut into two) in the lard until brown and add the salt and herbs.
2. Cover with the wine and water and simmer in a sealed pot (as above) for 1½ hours until tender.

The bones of pigeons were found in prehistoric middens at Glastonbury Iron Age lake village settlement in the west of England. There is a surprisingly amount of breast meat on even a small pigeon.

Hare Stew

250 g streaky bacon	
25 g butter	
1 hare that has been hung (or a rabbit)	
A bunch of chives	
1 kg chopped parsnip (there is a wild parsnip, but it can be confused with some very poisonous members of the umbellifer family of plants, so I would suggest using cultivated parsnips to be on the safe side)	
1 tsp salt	
Water	

Method

1. Fry the bacon in the butter in a pan slowly to release the fat, then add the hare or rabbit joints.
2. Cook until golden brown.
3. Add the chives, salt, the parsnips and enough water to cover.
4. Simmer for 1 hour over a stove or in a sealed pot as before. The parsnips caramelise and thicken the stock in this recipe. Very tasty, but be careful of the bones as they can be quite small.

Pork and Beer Stew

There is a wealth of quotations by the classical historians that the Celts in Europe loved wine and beer. Athenaeus mentions that 'the wheat beer prepared with honey, in Gaul was drunk by the poorer classes'. A lot of old country recipes also include beer, mainly to tenderise rather tough cuts of meat. Here are two for you to try. The tougher cuts of meat tended to be from older animals that, although they take longer to cook, have much more flavour than young animals.

1 loin of pork

28g lard

1 cooking apple or 5 chopped crab apples

A bunch of chives

500 g peas

1 tsp salt

1 pint brown ale

Method

1. Brown the pork in the pan with the lard.
2. Add the chopped apples, chives, salt and peas, and cover with the beer.
3. Seal in a pot or simmer slowly over the stove for 2 hours until the meat is tender.
4. Serve with chunks of bread to soak up the gravy.

Beef and Beer Stew

500 g stewing steak

28 g wholemeal flour

28 g butter

1 tsp salt

A large bunch of sorrel

56 g honey

1 pint of brown ale

Method

1. Dust the meat in flour and fry in the butter until brown.
2. Add the salt and chopped herbs.
3. Then add the honey and beer and seal in a pot.
4. Cook for 1½ hours until tender.
5. Serve, as before, with bread.

Bass Stew with Wild Mushrooms

125 g fatty bacon

A bunch of chives

A sprig of myrtle

A bowl of wild field mushrooms (*Agarius campestris*)*

1 large filleted fish

1 litre white wine

1 litre water

1 tsp salt

Method

1. Fry the bacon in small pieces with all the chopped herbs.
2. When soft, add the chopped mushrooms and cook for a few minutes.
3. Cut the fish fillets into pieces and put into the pot with the wine, water and salt.
4. Simmer over a low heat for 1 hour.

* A note of caution: please be careful when gathering wild mushrooms, unless you know how to recognise them. Many wild varieties of mushrooms can now be bought from supermarkets. I am sure that mushrooms would have been eaten in prehistoric times, and also possibly dried for winter use.

Cod and Oysters in Beer

3 ramson plants or 3 onions

A bowlful of fresh spring beech leaves (or use cabbage leaves)

A large piece of butter

1 kg cod

250 g oysters

1 litre brown ale

1 litre water

1 tsp salt

40 ml vinegar

A sprig of myrtle

Chunks of wholemeal bread chopped into cubes

Method

1. Fry the beech leaves and ramsons/onions in a pot with butter until soft.
2. Cut the cod into pieces and add to the pot along with the oysters.
3. Cover with the beer, water, vinegar and salt.
4. Drop in the sprig of myrtle.
5. Seal the pot with a lid and some flour paste. Cook by the fire for at least 12 hours.
6. Add the cubed bread – this soaks up the stock and thickens it. Eat immediately.

Soused Fish in Wine

Any fish can be cooked in this manner, although we only tend to cook herrings this way nowadays. Put some fish in a pot, add some mustard seed and some salt to taste. Cover with a mixture of water and white wine. Seal the pot and cook by the fire for 1 hour.

Cod with Mustard Sauce
(A Traditional Scottish Recipe)

A bunch of chives

1 kg fresh cod

1 cup milk

1 cup water

A little salt

3 tsbp butter

2 tsbp flour

A handful of crushed
mustard seeds

Method

1. Put the fish into a pan on top of the chives (this stops it from sticking).
2. Add the milk and water and salt and simmer gently for 10 minutes.
3. Remove the fish and chives and keep warm by the fire.
4. Melt the butter in a pan and stir in the flour and mustard seeds.
5. Add the fish liquor and stir until it thickens.
6. Pour over the fish and eat at once.

Mussel Stew with Dumplings

Stew

60 mussels

2 cups milk

Salt

Dumplings

1 cup water

A handful of fine oatmeal

Method

1. Wash the mussels and put into a large pan with the water, cover and heat until they open.
2. Strain the liquor into a basin and shell the mussels.
3. Lightly toast the oatmeal in a pan and put to one side.
4. Heat the milk with the mussel juice and add a little salt to taste.
5. Add the mussels but do not let them boil.
6. Put the oatmeal in a large bowl, add one cup of the stock stirring quickly so that it forms knots like small dumplings.
7. Add the oatmeal dumplings and the mussels and eat with lots of bread.

Rollmops

This simple method for pickling fish must have originated in ancient times to preserve the catch. Any fish can be pickled in this way, even salmon which tastes very good. Roll fish fillets with a ramson bulb or small onion inside. Place into a pot and add some mustard seeds and a little grated horseradish. Cover with white wine vinegar and leave for at least a week. The fish tastes good up to a month stored in this way. If stored longer, the fish meat still tastes good but becomes very soft.

CLAY-BAKED FOOD

There is some archaeological evidence for the practice of clay-baking foods: biscuit-fired clay fragments have been found in prehistoric cooking pits. These pieces of clay are not fragments of pottery but very friable rough chunks. At a Bronze Age settlement in Cornwall, large quantities of burnt clay were found in a hearth. Much of the clay was hard-baked and shapeless but some fragments had signs of smoothing by hand on them, and those pieced together formed a sort of shallow dish.

During my research into the possible methods of clay-baking foods, I have found that when a joint of meat is wrapped in river clay it is very difficult to carry to the fire to dry before baking. If, however, a piece of wood is placed underneath it, it makes the task much simpler. This wooden plank enables one to move and turn the clay-covered joint around the fire before baking. When the clay is dry the joint is dropped onto the fire and the wooden plank burns away during the cooking process. The clay has to be broken apart at the end of the allotted cooking time (usually two hours for a 3kg joint), but it is always soft and friable since river clay was used. This clay is freely available in most streams in northern Europe; it is not plastic enough to be used for pottery but is wholly adequate when it is used to clay-bake food.

This technique has been superseded by cooking 'en-croute' — wrapping meat in a flour and water dough — instead of wet river-bank clay. The clay-baking of food is not only a fascinating and novel way to re-enact the cooking techniques of our ancestors, but it is a delicious way to cook meat and fish, sealing all the flavour of the meat within the clay casing. The easiest way to do this is to dig a shallow pit in the open. Buy some raku clay, which is a clay that has had a lot of sand added to it so that it can stand the thermal shock of being placed in an open fire. Do not use ordinary ceramic clay that has no sand added, as it will explode when heated. A good supply of firewood is needed, preferably gorse wood if you can get it. This is by far the best wood for cooking, as it produces a very hot fire and does not spit. This wood is found in a large number of cooking pits on archaeological sites. Therefore, if you have a shallow pit, some raku clay and a large pile of wood, you are ready to clay-bake some meat or fish.

Clay-Baked Duck with Blackberries

Stuff a medium-sized duck with blackberries and season with salt. Wrap the duck in straw or dried grasses and tie securely with string. Cover the duck with an even layer of clay: this can be done by rolling the clay like pastry or just smearing it over in small pieces. The important thing is to seal the duck completely, leaving no cracks for moisture to escape. This done, place the duck onto a piece of wood and stand it by the fire to dry. Keep turning it every so often so that it dries evenly. When the top and sides are dry, roll the duck gently off the piece of wood and dry the underneath. Now carefully drop the duck into the side of the fire pit, keeping a good fire going. After an hour, turn the duck so the clay fires evenly around the bird.

After two hours, the duck should be ready. Using two forked sticks, lift the duck out of the pit and place on a wooden board. Crack open the clay casing and reveal (hopefully) a perfectly cooked duck with a blackberry sauce. As you can imagine, this is not an exact science – the thickness of the clay, the size of the duck and the heat of the fire all play an important part in the overall formula. Yet it is well worth trying, as the results can be absolutely delicious.

Clay-Baked
Lamb with Mint

Season a loin of lamb with salt and cover the exposed meat with as many mint leaves as possible. Wrap with straw or grasses and tie tightly with string. Cover with clay and bake in a fire pit as above.

Clay-Baked
Pork with Myrtle

Season a loin of pork with salt and cover with myrtle leaves. Wrap in straw or grasses as before and cover with clay. Cook as above.

Fish Baked in Clay

Any whole fish can be used; leave the
head on and gut them. Sprinkle with
celery seed (*Apium graveolens*) and salt.
Wrap in grasses as before and cover with
clay. Clay can be smeared directly onto
the fish if it is a thick-skinned, scaly
fish. If the clay is put directly onto a
thin-skinned fish like herring, it tends to
make the flesh gritty with the clay when
cooked.

Clay-Baked Trout with Ramsons

After gutting the trout, stuff it with chopped ramson bulbs (or leeks), butter and a little salt. Tie tightly at least two layers of ramson leaves or green leek leaves around the fish, and then cover in a flour and water paste. Tie on top of this a good layer of dried grasses and finally some silty clay (for instance, clay like that you might dig out of your garden) or foil. Cook the clay- or foil-covered fish in an open fire or in the oven for about an hour. Break the clay or remove the foil, and you will find that this fish is truly wonderful. The flour-dough coating seals the ramson or leek leaves in with the butter and the ramson bulbs, and it tastes like garlic-buttered fish. Look out for the wild ramsons in shady places and woodlands if you go for a walk in the spring; you will smell them long before you see them. This is a recipe well worth trying and would be a signature recipe for any top chef, if they were to make it!

King Carp Stuffed with Wild Plums

When demonstrating ancient cooking techniques in Poland, each day we were given a fish from the previous evening's catch from the lake to cook in clay. One day we were given a huge fish called a king carp, which must have weighed 7kg. We were cooking by a wild plum tree and, it being autumn, the wild sweet plums were ripe for the picking. So we stuffed this huge fish with wild plums, wrapped it in enormous burdock leaves, tied it with string and covered it with clay and cooked it by the fire for about three hours. When we broke open the clay, it was cooked to perfection and tasted wonderful. I had not tried king carp before and it tasted just like chicken.

Here is a shortlist of the fish remains found on prehistoric middens in northern Europe: eel, carp, pike, perch, trout, salmon, plaice, bass, mullet, cod and spurdog. At a recent excavation at Zamostie (Upper Volga, Russia), fish traps were found in the river silts; one of them was full of fish skeletons and is dated to the Mesolithic period (10,000 BC). No doubt something happened to the fisherman and he never retrieved his catch waiting for him by the riverbank. The trap was a conical-shaped basket made of split pine pieces, fixed by bands of tree–bark string.

Clay-Baked Wild Birds

The easiest way to cook wild birds is to not pluck them but to smear the wet clay directly onto the feathers. There is no need to tie straw or leaves onto the bird before adding the clay, as the feathers themselves act as a form of insulation. If, however, a bird with feathers on is hard to get hold of, then wrap in grasses as before. The only disadvantage to this method is that you cannot eat the skin of the bird; this comes away with the clay and feathers when it is cooked.

Clay-Baked Hedgehog

Although no one (I hope) is going to go out and hunt a hedgehog for food anymore, it is interesting to note that the traditional method the Romany people used to cook them is to clay bake them in an open fire. When the clay was broken off, the spines came off with it. It is said to taste rather like pork – hence its name.

SEASHORE

The Celts who lived by the seashore not only had a ready supply of iodine-rich salt but their diet was much more varied. Since Neolithic times, they could grow crops on the shoreline and hunt for game in the forests inland. In addition, they could harvest the shoreline vegetation, gather shellfish, and the many types of seaweeds that grow on the beach itself.

Laver (*Porphyra umbilicalis*) grows in the inter-tidal zone and rocky coasts around the British Isles, and is still eaten today in parts of Wales and Ireland. The seaweed is easily recognised and gathered as it has translucent purple fronds and crops up at all levels of the shore on rocks and stones. It can also be obtained from most health food stores. In Britain the traditional use for this plant is either as a sauce for mutton or as a laverbread.

Traditional Laverbread

First wash the laver in plenty of water and then simmer it in very little water until it is cooked (as you would with spinach), but be careful that it does not burn on to the pan. This puree is what is called laverbread. It can be stored in a jar in the refrigerator for a few days and used when required. The favourite way to eat it in Wales is to roll small pieces of this puree in oatmeal and fry it in bacon fat until crisp on the outside. It is then served with bacon for a supper or breakfast meal.

Sea Lettuce and Curd Cheese Fritters

Sea lettuce (*Ulva lactuca*) is quite common on British shores. It is found in rock pools attached to stones, is bright green in colour and really does look like lettuce. This recipe is packed full of protein and iodine.

A good bowlful of sea lettuce

1 cup soft cheese

1 egg cup of wholemeal breadcrumbs

Salt to taste

1 cup oatmeal

Bacon fat or butter for frying

Method

Wash the sea lettuce well and simmer in water until tender (about 30 minutes), then chop finely. Drain and add the soft cheese, egg, breadcrumbs and salt. Roll small pieces of the mixture into the oatmeal and fry in the bacon fat or butter. These fritters can be eaten hot or cold.

Shellfish

Prehistoric middens (rubbish dumps) near the sea contain large quantities of shells as a matter of course, usually mussels (*Mytillus edulis*), scallops or clams (*Pecten maximus*), limpets (*Patella vulgata*), cockles (*Cardium edule*) and winkles (*Littorina littorea*). Here is a recipe for winkle butter, which tastes remarkably like anchovy paste. It is possible that fish pastes such as these could have been traded with inland tribes for game.

Winkle Butter

(A note of caution: be careful that where you gather your shellfish is not on a polluted beach. Pick a beach that is far away from habitation and it should be alright, otherwise buy your winkles)

A bucket of edible winkles

250 g butter

28 g salt

After collecting the winkles, wash them in fresh water and soak in clean water overnight. Drain and plunge into boiling water, simmer for 15 minutes and drain. No comes the labor-intensive part (I find children love this job): with a large safety pin, point bent backward, proceed to pick the winkles out of their shells. Pull off the tough muscle and you should be left with brown coils from the inner shell: these taste delicious if you are fond of shellfish. Mash the winkles with the butter and salt. When you have a smooth paste it is ready to use. It is very good on toast or with bread hot from the oven.

Mussels and Bacon

This is a very simple way to eat mussels but very tasty. Fry some bacon in a pan then remove when crisp, put the mussels in the fat and shake over the fire until they have opened. Eat at once with the bacon.

Mussels in Horseradish Sauce

Cook the mussels in a pan until they open, then add some butter, a handful of mustard seeds and some grated horseradish. Cover these with single cream and serve at once.

Shellfish and Bacon Kebabs

Peel a willow stick and trim one end into a spike (or use a skewer). Skewer some oysters or scallops wrapped in sea beet leaves (or use spinach) with bacon, or any other combination – perhaps wild mushrooms, bacon and shellfish combinations. Roast them over a fire until cooked. For something really unusual and tasty, you could gather seaweed to wrap the shellfish in to give extra flavour to the kebabs. No seaweed is poisonous in Britain, but it is important that you pick it from an unpolluted beach.

Ash-Cooked Shellfish

Make a herb butter with chervil and a little salt or celery seed. Arrange any shellfish you have into the hot ash at the edge of your beach fire. As the shells open, add a small piece of the herb butter and eat at once with bread. Once experienced, you will not have a beach fire again without these tasty treats!

VEGETABLES

The endless variety of wild edible vegetation available to the northern European peoples, like the Celts and their forebears earlier in the Iron and Bronze Ages, could fill a book in its own right, so I will only list the vegetation that I have experience with cooking. When one talks about gathering wild vegetation from the hedgerows, most people imagine that one will be poisoned with the first mouthful, yet there are not as many poisonous wild plants as you might expect: most of these are in the umbellifer family. Whenever there is a poisonous plant which is similar to the vegetable proposed in the recipe, I will tell you. I will suggest various recipes for you to try and hopefully you will be inspired to create some new alternatives of your own. The list of wild vegetables is not in alphabetical order, but in the order of the ones I like best. I begin with one of the most common plants and yet one of the richest sources of vitamins and minerals, containing calcium, chlorine, iron, potassium, silicon, sodium and sulphur.

Nettle (*Urtica Dioica*)

One of the major uses of the nettle in prehistory was not for eating, but for making nettle fibre thread to be woven into fine cloth. From evidence found in the Neolithic settlements of Switzerland it is known that nettles were made into cloth before linen and wool. Fishing nets have been found made of spun nettle fibre that are so strong they would cut your skin if you tried to break them with your hands. The process to obtain this fibre is to strip the stem bark off the nettle in summer and then boil this in a solution containing wood ashes to remove the green parts. The fibres are then rubbed in dry clay to release the white fibre from the green filaments. What is left is nettle fibre, which is pure white and can be spun into thread with a spindle whorl. In Neolithic times a soft nettle cloth would have been very important, and the need to make a line for fishing strong enough to catch a large fish would have been essential. In early summer, therefore, there would be a lot of nettle gathering going on throughout Europe. As the stems are stripped of their leaves to be processed into thread, there would probably have been a lot of nettle-themed meals eaten at this time. This food would not be wasted as they had already gathered it for this other important activity. Nettle leaves could also have been dried and saved for medicinal purposes: if some nettle leaves are boiled in water for a few minutes, the liquid is a wonderful antiseptic for healing wounds. I have tried this remedy on a number of occasions and found that cuts bathed in nettle juice heal much quicker and leave no scar.

Creamed Nettles

Gather a large bowl of nettle leaves (wearing gloves) and wash them. Put them in a pot by the fire, or a pan on the stove and add a good piece of butter. Simmer over a low heat, stirring occasionally until tender. Strain, then put back into the pot with some salt, more butter and a little cream. Cook for 5 minutes and serve sprinkled with chives.

Nettle Oatcakes

Cook some nettles as above to the stage when you strain them. Put the strained nettles in a bowl, add a few chopped myrtle leaves, a little salt and an egg. Beat the mixture until smooth then add enough oatmeal to bind the mixture to a stiff dough. Leave to stand for 1 hour and then shape into small cakes. Fry in bacon fat or butter until golden on both sides. These cakes can be served hot with bacon or cold with cheese.

Fried Nettles

A plate of fried nettles sounds a little strange but tastes very much like fried seaweed. Pick some young nettle leaves, wash and dry them in a cloth. Heat a pan with some butter or bacon fat and add the nettle leaves. Fry until crisp. This can be crushed and added with salt to a wild salad as a flavouring.

Wild Salad and Nettle Crisps

A wild salad is still available in the countryside of Britain if you go out there and look for it with a good plant book. The main ingredient of a spring wild salad would be any combination of the following:

Jack-by-the-hedge (*Alliaria petiolata*)
Dandelion (*Taraxacum officinale*)
Bedstraw (*Galium sp.*)
Shepherd's purse (*Capsella bursa-pastoris*)
Sheep's sorrel (*Rumes acetosella*)
Hawthorn leaves (*Crataegus monogyna*) – in Spring only, as they are too tough by summer
Beech leaves (*Fagus sylvatica*)
Chives (*Allium schoenoprasum*)

Then add some of these flowers if available to sprinkle on top with some salt:

Clover (*Trifolium sp.*)
Chives (*Allium schoenoprasum*)
Gorse (*Ulex europaeus*)
Primrose (*Primila vulgaris*)
Violet (*Viola ordorata*)
Heather (*Calluna vulgaris*)
Elderflowers (*Sambucus nigra*)

For a really nice addition to the salad, add some crispy fried nettle leaves.

Rock Samphire
(Crithmum Maritimum)

This is my favourite wild vegetable. I eagerly wait for the spring when I can go down to the beach and collect it. Samphire grows on the rocks by the shore and is a succulent little plant with yellow umbellifer flowers. In sixteenth-century Britain there was quite an industry picking the Samphire and transporting it in barrels of brine to markets in London for sale there. It would have been a useful food source in the winter for prehistoric people too, who lived near the shorelines of Europe. It will keep fresh in strong salt brine for a year, and should be soaked in vinegar for a day before use.

Fried Rock Samphire

The simplest and nicest way to eat it is to boil it in water until soft and then drain and fry it in butter until crisp. This is a wonderfully interesting and tasty food to serve to friends at a barbecue. It can also be served just boiled with melted butter.

Samphire Pickle

Put the fresh leaves in a brine and leave for two days. Drain and put in a pot with some wild thyme and cover with red wine vinegar. Put the pot in a slow oven or by a campfire and bring slowly to the boil. When cold, store in pots until used. This is a recipe still used in the west of England, where this wonderful pickle is served with fish recipes.

Beer Samphire Pickle

This is also a traditional recipe, possibly coming to us from prehistoric times when home-made beer would have been plentiful. Wash the samphire very well in sour beer, then put it into a large cauldron or pot. Add a little myrtle and dissolve some salt in some more sour beer. Fill the pot with it, covering the samphire, and set it to boil by a fire until the leaves turn bright green. Drain and put into jars, then cover with vinegar mixed with a little honey.

Sow-Thistle (*Sonchus Asper*)

This herb is very rich in minerals and vitamin C, and was mentioned by Pliny. He said that Theseus dined off a dish of sow-thistles before tackling the Minotaur at Athena's suggestion. The seeds of the sow-thistle have been found by archaeologists at Iron Age sites in Denmark. The number of these seeds excavated increases at Viking sites: presumably its worth grew with its popularity.

Sow-Thistle Greens

Wash the leaves and put them in a pan without shaking the water off them. Add a piece of butter and cook until tender, then sprinkle with chives before serving. This makes a good addition to a mixed vegetable pot with dandelions and nettles. It is also good with salads if chopped, but a little bitter.

Sea Beet (*Beta Vularis*)

This plant is the ancestor of all modern beets such as beetroot, mangold, chard and spinach. The leaves have not changed much in cultivation, as the cultivator's attention was focused on the development of the larger root. The cultivated leaves have size and softness but have lost a lot of the flavour. It grows near the sea and can be easily identified by its thick and shiny, dark green leaves.

Sea Beet Greens

Wash the beet leaves well and put them over the heat in a pot or pan with a lid. When the leaves have all gone a darker colour, drain and serve immediately. The flavour is very like spinach and tastes as though it has been cooked in butter.

Sea Beet and Cheese Fritters

This is a way of making a savoury nutritious snack that can be eaten cold on a long walk, or for a journey wrapped in some uncooked beet leaves. Cook two handfuls of beet as above and drain. Chop the cooked beet and place in a bowl with a cup of wholewheat breadcrumbs, adding a cup of chopped hard cheese, such as cheddar, and a little salt. Bind with two eggs and shape into small cakes. Roll in rye flour and fry in a pan with some butter or bacon fat. These can be eaten hot — the cheese melts in little pockets within the fritters. These are very tasty and one of my children's favourites.

Sea Beet and Nut Fritters

Follow the recipe for beet and cheese fritters but add a cupful of chopped hazelnuts instead of the cheese. If fried in butter, this makes a good vegetarian fritter for a barbecue.

Fat Hen
(*Chenopodium Album*)

This is one of the most common seeds found on prehistoric sites apart from grain seeds. Its seeds are found in bog bodies in Saxony and Germany, as weel as in the Lindow Man in Britain and the Tollund Man in Denmark. It is very nutritious, as it contains more calcium and iron than cooked cabbage or spinach, and more calcium and vitamin B_1 than raw cabbage.

Fat Hen Greens

Cook as directed for sea beet and serve with butter for a spinach-like vegetable. It can also be used as a substitute in all the sea beet recipes. Fat hen grows in most northern regions and is easy to find, usually as a weed in a garden.

Sea Kale
(*Crambe Maritime*)

This grand plant grows on the shingle and sand on the edge of the beach. The plant used to be cultivated *in situ* and was tended by coastal dwellers from the spring until the early summer. When the first young shoots appeared in the spring, gravel and sand were piled up against them to blanch the shoots. This was done throughout the spring then the sand removed and the shoots harvested. The plant is very tough and bitter if it is not blanched in this way.

Sea Kale Shoots

Cut the shoots into manageable lengths and boil in salted water for 30 minutes. Serve with butter, like asparagus.

Wild Celery
(*Apium Graveolens*)

This plant grows in damp places and at the edge of reed beds. It is a very strong-smelling plant that grows up to 1–2ft high, with shiny yellow green leaves shaped like the garden variety. In an attempt to blanch out some of the strong flavour, it was brought into cultivation in medieval times in Britain. The leaves can be gathered and dried to add flavour to stews in the winter. The most valuable part of the plant is the seed, which, when crushed with salt, makes a wonderful spicy seasoning for all fish dishes. Warning: do be careful when identifying it for fear of poisonous imposters. When in doubt, use organic non-blanched varieties.

Chickweed
(*Stellaria Media*)

This plant has been in Europe since the late glacial period yet, to look at it, one would think it could not stand even a light frost. It is a succulent light green weed and not to be confused with the hairy dark green mouse ear chickweed which is not edible. Any gardener will recognise it instantly as a pest to be removed to the compost heap with all the other garden weeds. It is, however, a plant that was once sold at market stalls for salads, or for a wholesome tender vegetable. It is one of the few plants that is rich in copper, which is beneficial to a balanced diet. Wash this herb, dry it and add to a wild salad. This is a welcome addition in the early winter months as it is not affected by severe weather.

Chickweed Greens

Wash the plant and put it in a pot with a little butter and salt, and simmer until tender. Sprinkle with chives and serve.

Ramsons
(*Allium Ursinum*)

This member of the onion family is a beautiful sight when discovered by chance in the wild, yet one knows of its presence before one sees it because of its strong garlic smell. Another name for it is 'wood garlic', as it is found in damp shady places. The leaves are broad and the flowers a ball of white starry blossom. All parts of the plant can be used, but it is best eaten raw as it loses a lot of its flavour when cooked. Chopped fine in salads is best, or as a garnish to any savoury meal.

Marsh Thistle
(*Cirsium Palustre*)

This is the tall thistle that is found growing in marshland, looking like an elaborate candlestick standing tall among the sedge grasses. Although it looks unappetising, it is a wonderful vegetable. Handle with care when picking it though, as it has very sharp prickles. Also be careful when walking to cut it, as it tends to grow in very swampy conditions. The peeled stems of this plant, eaten raw, are like juicy celery and very good for a snack, or to be chopped into a salad. I am sure that when prehistoric people were walking into the marshes to gather sedge grasses to make hats and baskets, they would have had a snack of marsh thistle on a hot day.

Braised Marsh Thistle

If you like braised celery then you will like braised marsh thistle, as the taste and texture are almost identical. Pick the plant before the middle of the summer as it starts to become tough. Carefully peel the main stems of the plant and chop into sticks. Wash and put in a pot by the fire with a little butter and some salt. Simmer until tender and serve immediately

THE CELTS

Bistort
(*Polygonum Bistora*)

This plant also inhabits wet ground, mainly on hilly pastures and is native to most parts of Europe. In the north of England, the tradition of making a savoury pudding with this herb is still so strong that each year they have a Dock Pudding Making Championship. As you can imagine, there are many variations on this dish, so I will give you the recipe for the most traditionally made example.

Easter Ledge or Bistort Pudding

A good bunch each of bistort,
nettle and dandelion leaves

6 large blackcurrant leaves

1 leek or some ramson leaves

½ cup oatmeal

½ cup whole barley

Water to cover

1 tsp salt

1 egg

Bacon fat or butter to fry

Method

1. Wash, dry and finely chop all the herbs and the leek, and put into a bowl with the oatmeal and barley.
2. Add the salt, cover with water and leave overnight.
3. Put into a greased dish and bake slowly in an oven for 1½ hours.
4. Just before serving, add a beaten egg and return to the oven for a few more minutes.
5. An alternative method is to add the egg after soaking, slowly fry the whole mixture in bacon fat and serve with bacon.

Burdock (*Arctium Minus*)

If you have ever walked through an overgrown meadow in the late summer, you will recognise this plant. It is the one that deposits its round, ball-shaped burrs on any passing person, dog or horse. Its leaves are huge and look very much like a rhubarb. In Britain it is still made into a well-known and popular children's drink with dandelions. In Japan the plant is cultivated for the tough black roots, which are finely chopped and put into savoury dishes. It has a smell and flavour all its own so I will not try to describe it. It is the stems that are mostly used as a vegetable though. If picked in May (no later) the hard outer peel of the stem is stripped off to leave a thin, pencil-like stick., which is very good raw, chopped in salads or boiled and served with butter (like asparagus). The leaves are also very useful for wrapping fish before clay baking.

Silverweed
(*Potentilla Anserine*)

Silverweed is an almost universal plant that is native from Lapland to New Zealand, from China to Chile, and grows in most types of soil. The leaves of this plant are easily identified for they are silver and feather covered with downy white hairs. It is thought to have been a cultivated crop in prehistoric times. It is the roots that were harvested and eaten raw, boiled, baked or ground into a flour to be made into a bread. In more recent times, it has been used as a famine food as it is so abundant in the wild.

Pignut
(*Conopodium Majus*)

This slender umbellifer plant flowers in June and has leaves like fennel. It is always found in my part of the world and surrounds prehistoric sites in abundance. I am sure it was cultivated as it is one of the best root crops of the wild harvest. It was a popular wayside snack for children until recent times. The roots cannot be pulled up; one has to use a knife or finger to follow the slender stem underground and find the root. The root is the size and shape of a shelled hazelnut, and has a thin skin that is easily peeled away to reveal this juicy white ball. It can be eaten raw – a taste not unlike a cross between parsnips and hazelnuts – or it can be boiled or roasted to be added to savoury dishes.

Early Purple Orchis
(*Orchis Mascula*)

I am not suggesting that anyone goes out and digs up these now rare and beautiful flowers, but it is interesting to find out why they have in fact become so rare. The tubers of the orchis contain a starchy substance called bassorine, which is said to have more nutritive ingredients in it than any other single plant. One of these is said to be sufficient to sustain a man for a whole day. It is still widely used in the Middle East, being eaten raw or cooked, although it is mostly made into a drink by drying the tubers in the sun and grinding them into a rough flour. This flour is mixed with honey and stirred into hot milk until it thickens. In Britain a similar drink was made in Victorian times; it was mainly made with water, but spirits were added to it later. It was a drink for the workers and, in some cases, was made so thick it had to be eaten with a spoon. The early purple orchis cannot be easily cultivated as it depends on a peculiar association with fungi during its young stages and may take years to reach maturity. So the orchis for this popular life-sustaining food had to be gathered from the wild, hence the rarity of these plants today.

White Water Lily
(*Nymphaea Alba*)

This is the common water lily still found in sheltered ponds and lakes. It is the tubers of this plant that were eaten as a sustaining food in the past. These tubers can grow 6ft below the surface of lakes and ponds, which in the era of the Celts were probably infested with leeches. Therefore the tubers of the water lily, which I have not tried, must be either very sustaining or a great delicacy to merit the effort in obtaining them.

BREAD

The process of making grains into flours to bake bread was by using saddle querns (flat stones for grinding grains) in the Neolithic and Bronze Ages, and the more advanced rotary querns in the Iron Age. For the recipes using flour in this book, it is suggested that you use 100 per cent stone-ground wheat; however, in some large health food shops it is possible to find emmer, einkorn and spelt wheat flours. If you can get hold of these and want to be totally authentic, then use it wherever a recipe needs flour.

Sprouted grains would have been a common commodity in an ancient settlement during the spring, so the first recipes use wheat sprouts.

Wheat Sprouts

Take 125g of whole wheat grain, and soak it in water for 12 hours. Rinse and drain every day for about 10 days, keeping the container in a warm dark place. At the end of 10 days you will have a nutritious and tasty addition to a spring wild salad. The sprouts taste very much like liquorice and children will eat them in large handfuls – so ensure that you make enough to begin with. Any grain can be sprouted in this way, the best-known of course being the barley sprouts that produce malt for bread and brewing. Wheat malt is just as good, although not commonly made today, so here is a recipe for you to try.

Wheat Malt

Spread some sprouts on a tray and bake in a moderate oven (the prehistoric equivalent would have been a clome oven). Keep turning the sprouts as they brown: when they are evenly brown and crisp, take them out of the oven and cool. When cold, the wheat malt is ready to use. In prehistory it would have been ground between two flat stones then stored until use. A food processor will give you the same effect but is perhaps not quite as rewarding. The crisp, dry sprouts can be stored in an airtight container for many months until needed. In prehistory, a ceramic bowl sealed with a wooden stopper dipped into beeswax could have been used.

Malt Bread
(Unleavened, Makes Thirty)

500 g stone-ground flour

1 cup ground wheat malt

1 tsp sea salt

Water to mix

Method

Mix the dry ingredients together and add enough
water to make a soft dough. Shape into small round
flat cakes and cook on a hot griddle until firm.

Malt Bread (Leavened)

500 g stone-ground flour

1 cup wheat malt

1 tsp sea salt

1/2 cup fresh wild yeast
or a piece of starter
(or 28 g dried yeast)

Water to mix

Method

Mix the dry ingredients together, then add the yeast and enough water to make a soft dough. Knead the dough until smooth and springy, then leave it in a warm place for 3 hours. Knead again, then shape into two loaves and leave on a tray to rise for another hour. Cook in a moderate oven until brown (about 45 minutes).

Both of these recipes can be made omitting the malt for a plain brown bread.

Oat and Barley Bread

750 g medium oatmeal	
750 g barley flour	
250 g butter	
1 tsp sea salt	
Milk to mix	

Method

Mix the flours together then rub in the butter and add the salt. Mix to a soft dough with the milk. The oatmeal absorbs a lot of liquid, so do not make the dough too dry. Form into small cakes and cook on a hot griddle until firm and brown. This is a lovely savoury bread that is very good eaten with cheese.

Oatcakes
(As Still Made in Scotland)

500 g medium oatmeal
250 g stone-ground wheat flour
56 g lard
1 tsp sea salt water to mix

Method

Mix the flour and oatmeal together, add the salt and rub in the lard. Add enough water to make a dry dough and shape into flat cakes, then cook on a griddle until pale brown. When cold, spread with butter or top with a slice of cheese.

Sweet Bread

500 g honey
1.5 kg stone-ground flour
1 cup chopped hazelnuts
1 tsp sea salt
Milk to mix

Method

Mix all the ingredients together with enough water to make a soft dough. Shape into small flat cakes and cook on a hot griddle that has been dusted with flour (this stops them from sticking). When cold, spread with butter.

Rich Yeast Spring Bread

1 kg stone-ground flour

500 g butter

1 tsp salt

750 g honey

1 cup wild yeast or leaven
(or 28 g dried yeast)

3 eggs (preferably duck)*

Milk to mix

Method

Rub the butter into the flour and add the salt. Stir in
the honey, eggs and yeast. Add enough milk to make a
firm but soft dough and knead for five minutes. Leave
in a warm place for three hours then knead again. Place
on a baking tray and leave for another hour. Bake in a
moderate oven for one hour or until brown.

*Eggs should be thought of as a seasonal food only, so
when making this recipe think of it as a springtime treat.

Barley Bread with Beer

500 g barley flour	
500 g stone-ground wheat flour	
1 tsp salt	
250 g butter	
Beer to mix	

Method

Mix the flours and salt together and rub in the butter. Add enough beer to make a soft dough and shape into small cakes, then cook on a hot griddle until firm. This is a very light bread because of the addition of the beer and is very good with cheese.

Autumn Fruit Bread

1 kg stone-ground flour
A bowl of blackberries
1 tsp salt
500 g honey
Water to mix

Methods

Mix the flour with the blackberries then add the honey and water. Shape into small cakes and cook on a griddle, or make two loaves and bake in an oven for one hour.

Fresh Fruit Yeasted Bread

1.5 kg stone-ground flour

A bowl fresh elderberries

500 g honey

1 tsp salt

Water to mix

Method

Mix all the ingredients together and leave in a warm place for three hours. Knead and shape into two loaves and leave on a tray for another 2 hours before baking in a moderate oven for 1 hour. Serve with butter. This is a yeasted bread because of the natural wild yeast that lives on the elderberries.

BREAD CUPS

These recipes are for what the archaeologists call 'bread cups'. These carbonised bread cups have been found on Celtic sites in Britain and in Europe. They were made in prehistory by rolling out a simple flour and water dough into side plate-sized circles. These were then laid on top of hot, smooth, water-worn stones that had been in the fire, so that the bread cooked itself from the heat of the stones and formed itself into a bowl shape when removed. If you can get hold of some round, volcanic beach pebbles, put them on a tray in the oven until they are very hot, then place the dough over them carefully and cook for 25 minutes until they brown. If you have no stones, these can also be made by rolling the dough over some small metal pudding basins in the oven. After you have taken the bread off the stones, put them (using an oven cloth) into a bowl of cold water and you will see how easy it was to get hot water in prehistoric times! Once you have cooked your bread cups, you can add a variety of fillings. These are wonderful to take on a picnic, but if you are going to try and cook them authentically over hot stones, make sure that the stones are igneous or volcanic or they will explode when put in the fire. If you are in doubt about the stones, please find out before you try this, as sedimentary stones put into any fire can be very dangerous.

Here are a few suggested fillings for your cooked bread cups. I made the smoked fish, leek and nut ones for a *Time Team* programme and they were very popular with Tony Robinson and the film crew!

Plum, Honey and Venison Bread Cups

2 chopped venison steaks	
100 g honey	
500 g wild plums or small black plums	
28 g butter	

Method

1. Fry the plums in the butter, then add the finely chopped venison. When cooked, add the honey and cook for five minutes on a low heat so as not to burn the honey.
2. Fill the bread cups with this filling.

This is very good hot, but absolutely delicious cold for a picnic.

Bacon, Leek and Thyme Bread Cups

500 g leeks

250 g chopped fatty bacon

28 g butter

1 tbsp chopped fresh thyme
leaves

Method

1. Fry the bacon until crispy, then add the leeks,
   butter and finely chopped fresh thyme.
2. Simmer until the leeks are soft, then fill the bread
   cups with this mixture.

These are best eaten hot, as the leeks do not taste so
good when they are cold.

Smoked Fish, Leek and Nut Bread Cups (As Seen on TV)

500 g leeks

125 g chopped hazelnuts

50 g butter

250 g (any) smoked fish

50 g double cream

Method

1. Fry the nuts in the butter and add the chopped leeks, then cook until the leeks are tender.
2. Add the smoked fish and the cream and fill the bread cups with this mixture.

Sea Beet, Curd Cheese and Egg Bread Cups

500 g sea beet or spinach

200 g curd cheese
(cottage cheese is good)

2 large eggs

Salt to taste

Method

1. Cook the sea beet or spinach until it is soft and then chop finely.
2. Mix the cheese with the eggs and salt and stir into the beet, then cook until the eggs are set and spoon into the bread cups.

This is very good hot or cold as a vegetarian pie.

Hazelnut and Berry Bread Cups

300 g chopped hazelnuts
75 g butter
150 g honey
500 g mixed berries (any mixture e.g. blueberries, raspberries, blackberries and wild strawberries)

Method

1. Fry the chopped nuts with the butter and add the honey. Cook gently so as not to burn the honey and then add the berries.
2. Fill the cups with this mixture for a real treat.

DAIRY

There is little doubt that dairy foods were an important part of the prehistoric diet in northern Europe from as early as Neolithic times. Andrew Sherratt discusses the usefulness of milk as an addition to any diet, but looks on it as a secondary use of draught animals:

> Milk has several advantages. From a dietary point of view, it supplies the amino-acid lysine, which is missing in a cereal-based food. It contains fat, protein and sugar in a balanced form and is a useful source of calcium. Being liquid it is easily handled, and can be converted into a variety of storable products.

Archaeology now has evidence that milk products were consumed throughout Europe from Neolithic times, due to testing techniques developed at Bristol University, which recognises dairy-based fats preserved in pottery vessels. A high proportion of the bones excavated at many causeway camps in southern Britain were of calves. The cattle bones from Hambledon Hill are primarily those of older females and young calves. One archaeologist has interpreted these as the kill residue from a dairy herd kept in the settlement. This implies not just the consumption of veal, but the need for a large supply of milk for the community. The management of cattle herds continued through the Bronze Age and, in some ways, took on a ritual significance at various burial mounds. Perhaps the number of cattle consumed at the burial feast was an indication of a person's prestige and wealth, displayed by covering the tomb with the heads of the cattle.

Prestige of your own herds aside, here follow some advice on how to employ your own stores of milk.

Clotted Cream

You will need a large shallow pan; such as an enamel roasting tin.

Method No. 1 (Using Whole Milk)

Leave the milk in the tin in a cool place for a day until the cream rises to the top. Carefully carry the tin to the cooker, heat very slowly until a skin forms on the top and begins to wrinkle the surface. Remove from the heat and leave until cold. Carefully skim off the clotted cream the next day.

Method No. 2 (Using Cream)

Place the cream in a heatproof dish, into a tin filled with water and place directly onto the heat. Bring the water to the boil, then simmer for 20 minutes until the cream is scalded and a crust is formed on the top. Allow to cool overnight and skim off the clotted cream as above.

Butter

There are a few methods for making butter using whole milk and butter churns. The milk is left in the churn to ripen, then agitated until the butter floats to the top — hot stones heated in the fire can be added to speed up the separation. The making of butter is a fascinating process to watch, although we all take it for granted today. The best method is to start with double cream.

You will need a whisk, a bowl, a strainer, a small piece of butter-muslin or loose-weave cloth, and two wooden spoons. To truly re-enact the prehistoric process, try to make the whisk first from some green hazel or willow sticks. To begin with, strip the bark off the sticks with a knife. If this is done in the spring the bark will strip off in one piece as the sap is rising in the plant at that time of year – keep this bark for binding the whisk together. Then very carefully bend three of the sticks and secure them all at the cut end with the strips of bark or string. You have now made a very effective balloon whisk with which to make butter.

Method

1. Pour about 450g of the double cream into a bowl and begin to whisk. Continue until it is as stiff as you would use to fill a cake.
2. Keep on whisking until the cream looks like scrambled eggs and starts to look grainy in texture.
3. Now it becomes very hard to whisk and your stick whisk is put to the test. The mixture starts to make a watery noise. You will know what I mean when you hear it; it is quite difficult to describe but very noticeable. The butter becomes yellow as it starts to separate itself from the buttermilk, and at this stage the yellow butter forms a solid lump in the middle of the white buttermilk liquid.
4. Strain and save the buttermilk, perhaps to make some pancakes or sweet bread. The butter has to be washed with lots of fresh water to remove all of the buttermilk, otherwise the butter will go rancid

very quickly. If the butter is to be consumed that day, then this is not so important. The best way to wash it is to put it back into the bowl and stir with the spoon, adding fresh water every now and then, and then strain. Continue until the water runs clear.

5. Add a little salt to the butter and, with the two wooden spoons, squeeze small pieces of butter (extracting as much water as possible) and put it onto a plate. The butter is now ready to use.

Cheese

This simple method for making soft cheese is still being used in Europe today and allows for a variety of flavourings.

1 litre whole milk
A strainer cloth and string
250 ml beer, 250 ml sour cream or 28 ml wine vinegar for flavouring

Method

1. Put the milk in a pan and slowly bring to the boil.
2. Take the pan off the heat and add your flavouring, stirring until the curds and whey separate.
3. Place in the cloth and tie at the top to produce a straining bag for the curds.
4. Hang the bag over a bowl to drip for at least 1 hour.
5. Empty the bag and add a little salt to serve.

PUDDINGS

The first section of puddings are savoury accompaniments designed to be boiled in plain salted water – to emulate the unfortunate hunter who caught no game that day. These recipes are designed for outdoor campfire cooking, although they could be adapted by boiling the puddings and meat in a large pot over the stove. If hunting game or fishing on the seashore, the herbs for the pudding could be made with seaweeds with the addition of limpets and mussels for a savoury stock.

Following Seaweed Pudding, we move on to more conceptually familiar sweet puddings. The major sweetener in the Iron Age and Celtic periods was honey, yet there is also a large quantity of substances that can be added to food to make it sweet. There are many wild fruits that could have been used as sweeteners, such as blackberries, raspberries, cherries, plums, strawberries and bilberries. The reeds that formed the thatch for Iron Age dwellings were also a source of sugar. The fresh green stem is cut and left in the spring and a sugary sap forms around the cut; if this is left it can be picked off and eaten as a sweet. Reeds are known to soak up all kinds of organic compounds and are now used on an industrial scale to soak up pollution and heavy metals in water runoff from derelict Cornish tin mines. Therefore, if you live in a mining area, eating any part of a plant that absorbs heavy metals is not advisable. If you live in a chalk area, it would be safe to try this and see just how sweet the reed sap really is.

There are eggs in some of these recipes, which would have been a very seasonable food as it is very difficult to store them adequately. Any eggs would have been eaten, though probably the most common would have been duck eggs gathered from the marshlands. The community would have gathered the water reeds from the marshes every winter and spring to repair their thatched roofs, or for basketry. I should imagine that duck eggs would have been relished by the reed gatherers on their return to their settlements. In the Highlands of Scotland there is still a tradition of climbing the high sea cliffs to acquire seagull's eggs in the springtime. So if you wish your reconstructed Celtic meal to be truly authentic, then recipes containing eggs should be made only in spring and early summer. The rich spring grasses enriched the milk of the herds of cattle, so many of these recipes include cream.

Nettle Pudding

Method No. 1

| A bunch of sorrel |
| A bunch of watercress (*Nasturtium officinale*) |
| A bunch of dandelion leaves (*Taraxacum vulgaria*) |
| 2 bunches of young nettle leaves |
| Some chives |
| 1 cup barley flour |
| 1 tsp salt |

Method

1. Chop the herbs finely and mix in the barley flour and salt.
2. Add enough water to bind it together and place in the centre of the linen or muslin cloth.

3. Tie the cloth securely and add to the pot of simmering venison or wild boar (a pork joint will do just as well).

4. Leave in the pot until the meat is cooked and serve as chunks of bread.

Method No. 2

A bunch of sorrel
A bunch of dandelion leaves
A bunch of nettles
4 sprigs of mint (*Menta*) or wild marjoram (*Origanum vulgare*)
1 tsp salt
1 cup fine oatmeal
Water to bind (or if it is springtime, a hunter could have been lucky enough to find some wild birds eggs)

Repeat the process as for recipe No. 1 and cook in the pot.

Myrtle Pudding

At the Iron Age settlement at Glastonbury in England, the bones of black and red grouse and partridge were found. Of course, edible herbs are not easy to find on the top of moorland so the next recipe is a possible moorland pudding. On the moors in the west of England, there are many small stunted hawthorn trees, so I have added these to the recipe.

2 bunches of hawthorn leaves
A bunch of sorrel
A handful of gorse flowers (*Ulex europaeus*)
A small sprig of myrtle (*Myrica gale*)
1 cup oatmeal
1 tsp salt

Make as the prior two puddings, and add to the pot with your grouse or partridge.

Even though this meat is best left to hang for a few days, it still tastes pretty good when stewed in a pot with this pudding.

Seaweed Pudding

A few leaves of sea lettuce

A handful of sea beet

1 cup oatmeal

A bowl of limpets or mussels

1 egg

Method

1. Finely chop the sea lettuce and sea beet, add the oatmeal and bind with an egg or water.
2. Cook in the usual way, but add a bowl of limpets or mussels to the pot and use seawater to cook it in. As well as this, some fillets of fish could be added to make a hearty seafood stew with a herb pudding.

Seaweed Pudding with Blackberry Juice

I am sure that, in prehistoric times, every possible use would have been made of blackberries. Its sweetness and flavour would have been eagerly awaited during the winter, spring and early summer months. Carragheen, sometimes known as Irish moss, can still be picked from the mid shore around our coasts. As I mentioned earlier, though, do make sure the beach you pick it from is not polluted.

1 kg blackberries

1 litre water

125 g dried carragheen
(Irish moss)

Method

1. Bring the blackberries and water to the boil in a pot and simmer for 1 hour.
2. Strain and return fruit juice to the pot.
3. Add the seaweed (carragheen) and simmer for another 30 minutes until dissolved.
4. Pour into a bowl to set.

Seaweed pudding with Elderflowers

½ cup dried carragheen
[This can be bought at most
health food stores if you are
not inclined to search for
it on mid-shore rocks on
British and Irish beaches
and dry it yourself]

1 litre whole milk

A sprig of elderflowers

Method

1. Soak the dried seaweed in water for 10 minutes and drain.
2. Add this to a pan of whole milk and add a sprig of elderflowers.
3. Simmer for 30 minutes until the seaweed has dissolved, strain and pour into a bowl to set.
4. Leave until it goes cold when it will have set like a jelly.
5. Serve with a little honey, if desired, and some cream.

Beestings Pudding

'Beestings' is the name for the first milk that a cow produces after having a calf. Usually only for the first three days, it was an enjoyable and sought-after addition to the Celtic diet.

500 ml beestings

A pinch of salt

5 ml honey

Method

Place all of ingredients into a bowl and bake in a slow oven for one hour until solid. Store in a cold place overnight. Serve in small quantities (it is very rich) with a little honey. It tastes like a rich and creamy egg custard.

Junket

This is a less rich, traditional country pudding that I am sure is still well known throughout northern Europe. In our more recent history, before refrigeration and home freezers, people would eat seasonally. When a lot of calves were born to the herd, then recipes would be made to use up this plenty. My own experience when first owning a house cow shows how important it is not to waste the gallons of milk produced each day. One has to find recipes that include large quantities of milk just to keep up with it. My house cow produced 4 gallons of milk per day after calving, 1 gallon of which was thick, yellow cream. This recipe for junket is a good simple way of using the milk up. If you can get milk fresh from the cow, so much the better; if not, fresh whole milk from the dairy is just as good.

One litre of milk is put in a large bowl after being just warmed in a pan. Stir 10ml of rennet into this and leave to set. Serve as cold as possible in individual bowls with just a little cream and a spoonful of honey.

Pancakes

An easy, pleasant way to use up large quantities of milk and eggs is to make pancakes.

125 g wholewheat flour

500 ml milk

A pinch of salt

2 eggs

Method

1. Mix all of the ingredients together with a whisk until you get a smooth mixture.
2. Leave to stand for 2 hours, then cook in small spoonfuls on a hot griddle or pan.
3. Serve hot with honey and cream, or cold spread with butter and honey.

Hazelnut Pancakes

125 g wholewheat flour

500 ml milk

A pinch of salt

125 g honey

125 g roasted hazelnuts (stored
from the previous year)

Method

1. Mix all of the above together, adding the nuts after
   the mixture is smooth.
2. Cook in small spoonfuls or place into a large flat
   tray in the oven.
3. Serve in squares when hot with more honey and
   cream.

Sweet Dumplings

500 g wholemeal flour

2 eggs

125 g honey

Milk to mix to a thick batter

Method

1. Whisk the eggs, honey and flour together.
2. Gradually add the milk. Bring a pan of water to the boil or put a fireproof pot into the side of a campfire.
3. When the water is boiling, drop spoonfuls of the batter into the water.
4. Boil for 10 minutes until cooked and then ladle out and eat immediately while hot.

Hazelnuts could be added to this to make a richer dumpling.

Fruit Dumplings

500 g wholewheat flour
250 g wild fruit any of the
types mentioned earlier
Water to mix to a stiff batter

Method

Cook as Sweet Dumplings in a pan of boiling water
and serve hot with cream. This recipe has no eggs
in it, so it could have been made in the autumn and
summer when the wild fruits were plentiful.

Black Dumplings

500 g wholemeal flour or
oatmeal

250 g lard or pig fat

125 g honey

500 g blackberries and
elderberries

Water to mix to a moist
dough

Method

1. Rub the lard into the flour and add the fruit.
2. Mix in the honey and enough water to bind.
3. Place this dough into a large cloth, such as muslin, and tie it tightly into a bag, leaving a fold in the cloth so that the pudding can expand.
4. Drop the cloth into a pot of boiling water and simmer for 2 or 3 hours until firm and cooked through.
5. This should be a light pudding that has risen because of the wild yeast that is on the elderberries. Take out of the cloth, slice and serve with either butter or cream.

Oat and Wheat Nut Dumplings

250 g wholewheat flour

250 g fine oatmeal

250 g butter

125 g chopped roasted hazelnuts

250 g honey

A pinch of salt

2 eggs

Milk to mix

Method

1. Combine the flours and rub in the butter.
2. Add the hazelnuts and stir in the honey and eggs.
3. Add enough milk to make a soft dough.
4. Put into a large muslin cloth as previously and simmer in boiling water for 3 hours until cooked.
5. Take out of the cloth, slice and spread with butter.

Oat and Myrtle Cakes

3 medium sized leeks or ramsons

125 g lard

A good sprig of myrtle

1 tsp salt

1 cup medium oatmeal

1 cup water

Method

1. Fry the chopped leeks in the lard until soft.
2. Add the chopped myrtle leaves, salt and oatmeal.
3. Cook for 1 minute, stirring all the time.
4. Add the cup of water and cook until all of the water is absorbed by the oats.
5. Leave it to go cold, then shape into small cakes and brown on both sides on a hot stone or griddle.

This could be made with butter instead of lard for a vegetarian version.

Sweet Bean Cakes

These are a family favourite.

250 g butter

500 g wholewheat flour

500 g Borlotti beans (mashed with a fork)

500 g honey

125 g chopped hazelnuts

Method

1. Rub the butter into the flour and add the beans.
2. Stir in the honey and hazelnuts.
3. Cook spoonfuls of the mixture on a hot griddle until light brown on both sides.

This could be made at any time of the year because all the ingredients are easily stored. They are very nutritious and make a great snack.

Poppy Seed and Blackberry Cake

This is based on a continental recipe for poppy seed cake, using blackberries instead of candied peel.

1 ½ cups poppy seeds

6 eggs

1 cup honey

½ cup blackberries or any other fruit

Method

1. Grind the poppy seeds between two stones or in a blender until you have flour.
2. Beat the egg yolks until thick and, while beating, gradually add the honey.
3. Stir in the blackberries and the ground poppy seeds.
4. Beat the egg whites until stiff and fold into the mixture.
5. Pour it into a lightly floured and greased dish and bake in a moderate oven for about 50 minutes.
6. Allow the cake to cool in the dish, serve with fresh whipped cream.

Fruit and Cream

The simplest way to enjoy the wild fruit harvest is to just eat the fruit in a bowl and pour over some cream. The sweetness is provided by the fruit itself and just as relished today in our over-processed age as I am sure it was in the distant past.

Prehistoric Solstice Feast

OF COURSE IT would not have been a Christian festival during the Celtic period, it would have been a Winter Solstice festival. This was a very important festival for the Celts because it meant that the days were getting lighter again.

Here follows a course-by-course approach to a Winter Solstice Feast to keep your spirits up until Spring arrives.

Breakfast on Feast Day

A bacon sandwich! For a feast day treat they might have indulged themselves with a slice of wholesome bread, liberally spread with butter and eaten with lots of bacon crisped on stones by the fire.

Any Spit-Roasted Meat (Apart From Chicken)

A large spit-roasted boar or deer would have been a favourite if the hunters had been successful. Chickens in the Celtic period, however, were very small bantam-like birds and not a particularly special meal.

Smoked Fish Stew

This is of course a store-cupboard meal, as there would have always been one or two of their cows in milk at that time to provide the cream for this appetising dish. I have made this so many times in outdoor conditions and it is always delicious and so quick to make.

125 g bacon
2 leeks
500 g of any mixed smoked fish
1 litre milk
300 ml cream
2 tbsp chives
1 tsp salt

Method

1. Fry the bacon until the fat comes away from it and add the chopped leeks. Cook until tender.
2. Add the fillets of fish and cover with the milk.
3. Slowly cook in a pot near the fire until the fish is cooked, which takes about 30 minutes.
4. Pour in the cream, along with the chopped chives and salt.

This is very good eaten with chunks of home-made bread for dipping.

Whole Salmon Baked in Clay

3 kg salmon
2 tbsp celery seed
1 tsp salt
A bunch of sorrel
A bunch of chives
Lots of long grass (green or dried) string
Clay

Method

1. Stuff the salmon with the herbs, salt it and sprinkle with celery seed.
2. Cover the fish in grass, either dried or fresh green grass can be used.
3. Tie it tightly with string.
4. Smear a plank of wood with clay and put the fish on it, then cover it completely with the rest of the clay.

5. Put it next to an open fire or BBQ to dry the clay, and then slide it off the board and drop it into the fire. Build the fire or BBQ over it and keep it going for at least 1½ hours.
6. Break open the clay covering and remove the grass and enjoy. This is the only way my son Dominic will eat salmon!

If you do not want to use an open fire, then follow the instructions up to stage 3, cover it with foil and bake in an oven for the same amount of time. If you are eating the salmon cold then leave it in its casing of either clay or foil until it has cooled and it will be so deliciously juicy. I have never been able to do this successfully because whenever there is a group of people around me they always eat it all before it has a chance to go cold!

Fried Crab Apple and Honey Bread Cups

Honey was always saved for festivals in prehistory as it was mostly wild honey and not always easy to come by. This recipe makes good use of it though.

1 kg crab apples or cooking apples (cored and sliced)

75 g butter

200 g honey

200 g brown breadcrumbs

Ready-made bread cups

Method

1. Fry the apple slices in the butter until the apple starts to brown.
2. Drain and pour the remaining butter in the breadcrumbs with the honey and mix well.
3. Put a layer of the honey and breadcrumbs in the cups then a layer of the fried sour apples, and then top with more breadcrumbs.
4. Eat either when hot or cold with cream. They are very sweet, but with the sour centres they are incredibly moreish.

Bread Baked in Honey

In one of the ancient Irish texts about the Feast of Bricriu, it says that 'He gathered food for a whole year, and he built a house at Dun Rudraige from which to serve it.'

There exists a list of the food that was prepared for this monumental feast, and the last part of the menu stated '100 wheaten loaves baked in honey'. It seemed strange to me that this particular quotation did not describe 100 wheaten loaves with honey, or 100 wheaten honey loaves. It described the loaves as baked in honey. At an open-air cooking demonstration, I decided to try this wheaten loaf baked in honey in a stone bank oven. This is an oven that is cut into an earthen bank and lined with large granite stones. A small hole is left at the back of the oven to allow the smoke to escape when a fire is lit inside.

After a fire has been roaring for about an hour in the oven, the ashes are brushed out and a bowl containing the fresh fruit bread dough floating in honey was put into it. Any fruit-laden bread dough recipe can be used for this, but I found one with fresh wild plums that is very nice. I poured a litre of runny honey into a ceramic bowl and dropped the dough into this in one piece. I have to say that I was convinced the honey would burn when it was put into this very hot oven. The stone was placed to seal the oven and grass turf was put over the cracks to seal the heat in. After two hours, however, the oven door was opened and to my amazement the fruit bread was cooked to perfection. The honey had not burnt at all and had partly seeped into the bread dough, making a delightfully sticky prehistoric equivalent to a Rum Baba without the rum! Well worth trying at a winter bonfire party or in your oven at home for a Solstice feast.

Honey Drinks

The Celts always sweetened their stored beer or fruit wine with honey just before drinking it so, in a way, everything had a meady taste. At festival time they would have probably put more honey into the beer as a treat. So buy some real ale and add a few tablespoons of honey to it. Heat it in a pot from within with a hot stone or a clean fire poker, and sprinkle some fresh herbs of your choice into it for a hot, festive honey drink.

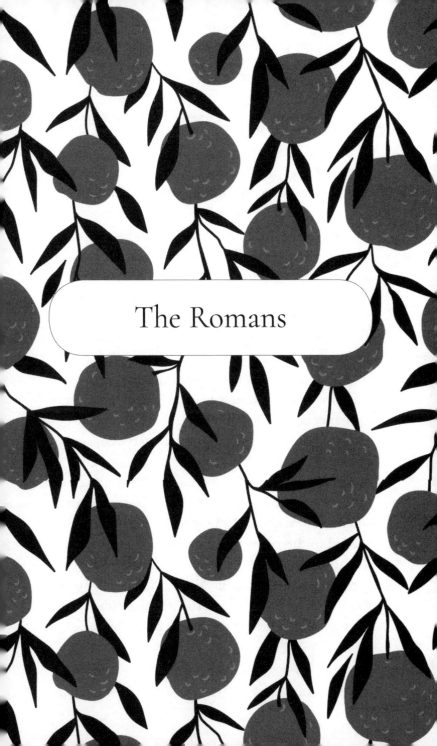

The Romans

THE ROMANS WERE the first people to colonise Britain in the true sense of the word, stamping their architecture and culture on those that lived here before. After the initial resistance of the Celts to the invasion, the Romans put into action their method of taking over the minds and souls of the peoples they invaded. Firstly they gave them jobs in their country villas and cities and invited them to share some of the exotic foods they imported. Then they put on mass entertainments for the workers, including the circus, gladiator fights and chariot races. Large numbers of Celts were therefore slowly tempted into living this British version of the Roman way of life. The Roman settlements, however, did bring great changes to our countryside. They brought with them the concept of planting fodder crops: crops primarily designed to be fed to animals to keep them healthy throughout the winter. Previously in the Celtic settlements, when the grazing and hay ran out, the animals not needed for breeding were slaughtered and the meat was preserved for the winter. This practice was incorporated into their Winter Solstice festival, when they acknowledged the darkest time of the winter and celebrated the return of the light.

As well as fodder crops, the Romans brought most of the plants we still grow in our vegetable patches today. If one reads Pliny's *The History*, it is just like a TV gardening book you might buy at Christmas. He details all you need to know about growing vegetables and even how to make pelleted seeds. I thought we had invented that in the 1970s, but no, Pliny describes how one should push a seed into a sheep or goat dropping and then plant it in the ground, ensuring that it has enough food surrounding it to supply the germinating plant.

Vegetables were the staple food of most Romans, and so it was incredibly important to them to improve their gardening techniques. Their favourite vegetable was the cabbage, of which they grew five distinct varieties. Root vegetables and onions were important too, as they could be preserved throughout the winter. While meat was enjoyed, it was outclassed by fish, egg and vegetable recipes.

The spice markets of southern Asia were the focal point of the Roman traders in their desire to collect more and more exotic spices for the tables of the Roman nobility. These spices became common and plentiful in Britain as the Roman occupation became established. Pepper, cinnamon, cumin, nutmeg, ginger and cloves were transported by ship from India, Sri Lanka, the Bay of Bengal, the Spice Islands and China. The flow and frequency of this trade at the time of the Roman Empire was not replicated again in Britain until the return of the Crusaders in the eleventh century.

In Roman gardens they grew thirty-two varieties of apples, thirty-four varieties of pears and forty-four varieties of figs. This was incredible, as even our most prestigious grocers could not contemplate stocking thirty-four varieties of pears, for instance. Peaches came from Persia, pomegranates from Tunisia, apricots from Armenia and cherries from the Near East. These fruits would have been imported for the Roman nobility that colonised Britain, but there would always have been leftovers for the servants too, I am sure. Those strange fruits and spices would have been a complete revelation to the local British workforce that maintained and ran their villas.

Apart from potatoes, tomatoes and sweetcorn they grew most of the vegetables we grow today. But that is where the similarity stops. The high-ranking Romans felt that they were too sophisticated and refined to just boil some carrots, say, and eat them with a sprinkling of salt. They had to change the look of their food to make a vegetable look like a fish and vice versa. They would instruct their servants go to considerable lengths to hide the natural forms of their foodstuffs. They would not even sprinkle their food with salt; as that was far too simplistic for their palates, they had to make a fermented fish sauce called *Garum* or *Liquium* with which to season their food. Thanks to the wealth of literature left by the Romans, it is reasonably easy to find recipes for the Roman people.

The average person in a Roman British town would live in an apartment just as most Italians do today, and these apartments would not have had kitchens. So people would eat a light breakfast of bread and fruit and at midday they would eat cold meat or fish with bread. In the evening, however, they would go and get a takeaway from the wealth of street-fronted establishments in their towns. In Pompeii there is a good example at a place called Arsellina's Tavern; this street-fronted bar had sunken pots in the counter to serve steaming hot food to the passing trade. The type of food served in these pots could be something like lentil stew or lamb in plum sauce or pork and leek sausages – all of which are recipes for you to try in this chapter. The lentil stew, which incorporates cumin powder and fresh dill, does sound a little odd, but I have tried it many times and it is really delicious. Most of us think our takeaway city culture in Britain is a very modern phenomenon, but it was actually going on 2,000 years ago!

A Roman called Marcus Apicius wrote a cookery book that shows in detail what the Roman nobility ate. He was a decadent gourmet during the first century AD. He was said to actually teach haute cuisine, and his love of fine foods was actually his downfall in the end, for his lavish dining extravaganzas had made him bankrupt and he was said to have taken his own life with poison during one last fantastic meal, rather than eat like the poor people.

A poet of the time, Martial, wrote this poem about Apicius's demise:

After you'd spent 60 million on your stomach, Apicius,
    10 million still remained,
An embarrassment, you said fit only to satisfy mere hunger
    and thirst:
So your last and most expensive meal was poison …
Apicius, you never were more than a glutton than at the end.

I think that poor Apicius would have been delighted to know that his own recipes were still being made over 2,000 years later. Another typical Apicius tale is this one, related by a historian called Athenaeus:

> Apicius of extraordinary wealth ... passed his time for the most part eating very costly prawns of the region of Campania ... He happened to hear that prawns also grew enormous size off the Libyan coast [all of Africa was called Libya at the time]. Accordingly he set sail that very day. After suffering from storms during the voyage across the open sea he drew near to the land.

Apparently, when he got there he found the prawns were no bigger than the ones he ate in Italy, so he had the boat turned around and went straight home – such was his dedication to his palate.

Just as a point of interest on the Roman food front, there has been some research from the University of Vienna on the diet of Roman gladiators. They tested the bones from a gladiator graveyard in Ephesus in modern day Turkey, and were shocked to discover that the diet of those prime fighting men was mainly made up of vegetables and barley – just carbohydrates, with very little, if any, meat proteins. The reason for this was found in historical accounts: the gladiators had to have a good layer of fat on them in order to keep fighting once wounded. A thin gladiator would be dispatched too quickly, as glancing blows of the sword would be able to cut into their internal organs. The fat layer apparently let the fighters carry on long after they were wounded. This diet would have given the gladiators a serious calcium deficiency, but historical accounts say that they were made to drink bone ash to keep their bones strong. Somehow one imagines the Hollywood versions of the gladiators as slim muscular men, rather than ones carrying a good layer of fat to protect them in battle!

ROMAN INGREDIENTS FOR COOKING

The famous Roman fish sauce, *garum* or *liquamen*, was made in factories around the Empire and transported to all corners of it in amphora to season savoury food. It was made by putting the entrails of oily fish into great vats with salt and fermenting it for six months in the hot sun. This sauce was used in almost every Roman recipe. The simplest equivalent is nam pla, the Thai fish sauce that is readily available in Britain today.

In a lot of the original recipes they use rue, fleabane and other mildly toxic herbs to add bitterness to dishes. The most exact equivalent is angostura bitters, as it will do the same job without running the risk of poisoning yourself!

Boiled wine is used in a lot of recipes too, so if you are planning on doing a lot of Roman cooking it would be best to make a batch. Just boil either red or white wine until it is reduced by half, and then bottle it for future use.

COLD FOOD

This food can be prepared well in advance to make a wonderful Roman feast for your friends to enjoy. All the Roman desserts were cold and these can be enjoyed at any Roman banquet. In the Roman period, homemade desserts were really rare, and so a huge bowl of succulent fruit (especially peaches, fresh figs and grapes) is actually more authentic, and is a definite must on any buffet table.

Boiled Eggs and Anchovies

This is a very simple recipe, but the Romans did tend to play with their food, making it look like it was something else. They were known to make hare or kid or sometimes chicken livers into the shape of a fish. They made vegetables look like meat in the same way. For a TV programme, I made this recipe into a fish shape, and this would look good on a buffet table.

8 hard-boiled eggs
1 tin anchovies
50 g raisins
50 g pine nuts
1 tbsp vinegar
1 tbsp oil
A handful of radicchio lettuce leaves
Flaked almonds and one pea for making a fish shape)

Method

1. Chop the eggs and the anchovies and mix in the raisins, pine nuts, vinegar and oil until it is like dough.
2. Lay some radicchio lettuce leaves on a platter and put the egg dough onto it. Shape it to look like a large fish.
3. Layer the flaked almonds along the body of the fish to replicate scales and press a green pea on it in place of its eye.

Bread Salad

This is a great accompaniment for any cold Roman savoury dish, or could be served on a buffet in slices.

1 loaf of white bread
100 ml mild vinegar
100 ml water
250 g grated cheese, such as Cheshire or Caerphilly
1 tbsp honey
3 cloves garlic
A pinch of pepper
A small sprig of mint
A large bunch of fresh coriander
75 g chopped spring onions
30 ml olive oil
50 ml white wine vinegar
3 tbsp water
Salt to taste

Method

1. Remove the crust off the top of the loaf and hollow it out.
2. Soak the bread you have taken out with vinegar and water and set it aside.
3. Cover the bottom of the loaf with half the grated cheese.
4. Chop the herbs and mix with the other ingredients.
5. Add this to the bowl of soaked breadcrumbs and mix well together.
6. Fill the loaf with the ingredients and top with the rest of the cheese.
7. Chill well before serving in slices.

Scallop Rissoles
(Made to Look Like Parsnips)

24 scallops

¼ tsp pepper

1 tsp fish sauce

1 egg beaten

50 g flour

Salt and pepper to taste

Sprigs of rosemary leaves for decoration

Method

1. Quickly fry the scallops in some oil. Chop the cooked scallops finely and put in a bowl.
2. Add the pepper, fish sauce and the beaten egg.
3. Mix well and shape into cones the shape of a parsnip, or just rissoles if you are not shaping it.
4. Roll in seasoning flour and fry gently in olive oil until browned on all sides, keeping the shape intact.
5. Stuff some sprigs of rosemary leaves in the end to replicate the parsnip tops and serve as a starter or on a cold buffet.

Sweet Date Chicken Salad

500 g cooked chicken meat cut into cubes

¼ tsp pepper

2 tbsp chopped parsley

200 g chopped dates

A bunch of chopped spring onions

150 ml wine

1 tbsp white wine vinegar

Method

1. Put the dates, pepper, wine and vinegar in a pan.
2. Simmer gently until the dates have absorbed the liquid.
3. Stir in the onions, parsley and the cooked chicken.
4. Put on a serving dish and serve cold.

Onion Relish for Ham

4 large onions

A handful of fresh thyme

A handful of fresh oregano

125 g chopped dates

2 tbsp honey

2 tbsp vinegar

75 ml boiled wine

1 tbsp olive oil

2 tbsp onion stock

Method

1. Boil the onions in lots of water and drain saving a little stock.
2. Chop the cooked onions finely when cold.
3. Add all the other ingredients and chill for 24 hours before use.
4. Serve with ham or cold fish.

HOT FOOD

The origins of the Italian lasagne can clearly be seen in this recipe from Apicius's book.

The Original Lasagne

Meat or fish sauce

500 g cooked chicken, filleted fish or pork

3 eggs

¼ tsp pepper

1 tsp celery seeds

300 ml stock (chicken, fish or pork)

150 ml sweet wine

150 ml dry white wine

3 tbsp olive oil

Flour to thicken the sauce

125 g pine nuts

Dough

500 g flour

250 ml olive oil

1 tbsp salt or fish sauce

Water to mix

Method

1. Make a soft dough with the flour, oil and water.
2. Roll out into four circles the size of the oven-proof dish it is to be cooked in and set aside.
3. Mix the meat or fish with the other ingredients (apart from the eggs) in a pan and bring to the boil.
4. Simmer for 20 minutes, adding more stock if needed to keep it liquid.
5. Whisk in the eggs to thicken the sauce.
6. Lay one of the dough circles in the base of the dish and ladle some of the meat or fish sauce over it.
7. Repeat this process until you finish with the dough on the top.
8. Make some holes in the top crust and brush with beaten egg and sprinkle with pepper.
9. Bake slowly in an oven for 1 hour until all the dough layers are cooked between the meats.
10. Leave to stand for 30 minutes after taking out of the oven and cutting into squares.

Roman Army Lentil Stew

100 g green lentils
1 medium onion
125 ml red wine
1 tsp cumin seeds
1 tsp dried dill or a bunch of fresh dill
A sprig of thyme
A sprig of oregano
A handful of fresh parsley (optional)
1 tbsp olive oil
Black pepper and sea salt to taste

Method

1. Slice the onion thinly and fry gently in olive oil until soft and just beginning to turn golden brown.
2. Add 600 ml of water, the red wine and the lentils.
3. Using a pestle and mortar, grind the cumin and aniseed together and add this to the mixture along with the dill.
4. Bring the mixture to the boil and simmer for 45 minutes, or until the lentils have cooked through. Make sure that all the liquid has boiled away so that the lentils are almost dry.
5. Stir in the finely chopped thyme and oregano. Mash lightly with a fork and tip into a bowl. Garnish with chopped parsley or thyme and serve.

Pork and Leek Sausages

We all think of pork and leek sausages as a modern invention, at least I did until I saw Apicius's recipe. It is spicier and has ground almonds in it, but it is still a pork and leek sausage. Interestingly, Apicius suggested these sausages were boiled in pork stock, like frankfurters, and once cooked, they were browned under a grill.

450 g minced pork

225 g fine breadcrumbs

2 leeks, finely chopped

125 g cooked bacon, chopped

50 g ground almonds

1 tsp pepper

2 tsp celery seeds

1 egg beaten

A saucepan of pork stock

Sausage casings

Method

1. In a bowl mix the pork, breadcrumbs, leeks, bacon and almonds well.
2. Add the celery seed and pepper and bind with an egg.
3. Put into casings or shape into sausage shapes.
4. If using casings, boil in stock for 30 minutes then brown in the oven.
5. If not using casings, roast on a tray in a hot oven for 30 minutes.
6. Serve hot or cold.

Mushrooms in Honey

25 g dried porcini
mushrooms

2 tbsp red wine vinegar

1 tbsp clear honey

Salt to taste

Method

1. Put mushrooms in a bowl, cover with boiling water
   and allow them to soak for 1 hour.
2. Pour the mushrooms and liquor into a pan, add the
   honey and vinegar, and bring to the boil.
3. Cover and simmer for half an hour.
4. Season with salt and serve. This mushroom mixture
   goes particularly well with game.

Spiced Squash
(To Look like a Crab in Seaweed)

1 medium-sized squash

½ tsp pepper

1 tsp ground cumin

1 tsp fresh ginger

2 drops angostura bitters

1 tbsp wine vinegar

300 ml boiled red wine

300 ml stock

1 small squash to cut into crab claws to decorate the dish (parboil it before you cut it so it is not too brittle to shape)

2 raisins for the crab's eyes

1 small green cabbage like a Savoy

Method

1. Cut the squash flesh into chunks and boil until cooked.
2. Strain, keeping the stock, squeeze out the liquid and put it in a fresh pan.
3. Add to the pan all the other ingredients and simmer for 30 minutes or until all the liquid is absorbed.
4. Serve at once unless you intend to shape it like a crab.
5. If you are going to shape it: put on a large serving dish and shape it into the body of a crab using the parboiled squash crab claws. You just have to make it into an oval dome with the claws coming out of it. Use the raisins for the eyes and put it on a platter of finely shredded boiled cabbage. Eat cold with cold meat or with fish and bread.

Spring Greens with Cumin

500 g spring greens

1 tsp cumin seeds

2 tbsp olive oil

300 ml stock

150 ml wine

1 tbsp fish sauce

Method

1. Shred the spring greens finely, including the stalks.
2. Heat the oil in a pan and add the cumin seeds, frying until they start to crackle.
3. Add the shredded spring greens to the pan, stir well and cook for a further 5 minutes.
4. Pour in the stock and wine and simmer until cooked and the liquid has evaporated.

PLUM SAUCES

Here are three different plum sauces for venison, lamb and duck. They are all very different and well worth trying:

Plum Sauce for Venison

2 kg roasted venison joint

A handful of chopped lovage or celery leaves

2 tbsp parsley, finely chopped

500 g fresh plums, chopped

1 tbsp honey

150 ml red wine

1 tbsp vinegar

1 tbsp fish sauce

2 tbsp olive oil

250 ml stock

Method

1. Chop and stone the plums, then cut into small chunks.
2. Put all the ingredients in a pan and stir slowly over the heat until the plums are soft.
3. Reduce the heat, cover and cook slowly for 1 hour.
4. Pour into a sauce boat and serve with roast venison.

Plum Sauce for Roast Lamb

2 kg roasted lamb

½ tsp ground ginger

½ tsp pepper

2 tbsp olive oil

½ tsp dried savoury

1 tsp finely chopped fresh rosemary

225 g stoned and finely chopped fresh plums

1 finely chopped large onion

150 ml red wine

150 ml stock

2 tbsp wine vinegar

Method

1. Roast the lamb in the usual way.
2. Prepare the sauce by frying the onion in the oil and stir in the herbs. When the onion is soft, add the other ingredients, apart from the vinegar.
3. Simmer gently for 1 hour.
4. When the roast is cooked, put it on a platter and pour the hot sauce over it. Drizzle the vinegar over the sauce and serve.

Plum Sauce for Duck with a Pastry Crust

1 large duck

A pinch of peppercorns

250 g shallots

A large bunch of lovage or
young celery leaves

½ tsp cumin

½ tsp celery seeds

70 g stoned plums

50 ml red wine vinegar

50 ml fish sauce

50 ml grape juice

30 ml olive oil for sauce

200 g flour

Olive oil for pastry

Method

1. Make pastry with the flour and enough olive oil to bind the flour together. If too dry, add a few drops of water.
2. Season this with salt and pepper and cover the duck in a layer of pastry.
3. Place in a roasting tin and roast for 2 hours in a moderate oven.
4. Meanwhile, place all the herbs in a mortar and grind with a pestle.
5. Add this to a pan with the plums, vinegar, fish sauce, grape juice and 30ml of olive oil.
6. Cook until the plums are tender.
7. Strain the sauce and pour over slices of duck and pastry.

Date and Herb Sauce for Poached Tuna

3 tuna fish steaks

¼ tsp pepper

½ tsp celery seeds

¼ tsp thyme

1 finely chopped onion

125 g chopped dates

1 tbsp honey

1 tbsp vinegar

1 tbsp fish sauce

1 tbsp olive oil

150 ml water

Method

1. Poach the tuna fish lightly in the usual way.
2. Sauté the onion in the oil until tender.
3. Add the herbs and cook for another minute.
4. Mix in the other ingredients and stir well.
5. Add the water and simmer until the water has been absorbed.
6. Spread this mix over the tuna steaks and serve immediately.

Stuffed Herrings
or Stuffed Trout

2 cleaned fish with the heads
and tails left on

¼ tsp pepper

½ tsp cumin seeds

1 tbsp chopped fresh mint

200 g chopped walnuts

1 tbsp honey

2 tbsp olive oil

4 tbsp boiled wine

2 tsp fish sauce

Method

1. Clean the fish, leaving the head and tail on.
2. Mix together the cumin, pepper, mint, walnuts and honey.
3. Stuff the fish with this mixture and put it in an ovenproof dish with a lid on. Bake for 35 minutes until the fish is cooked.
4. Mix together in a dish the olive oil, wine and fish sauce and heat through in a pan.
5. Put the fish on a serving dish and pour over the olive oil, boiled wine and fish sauce dressing and serve.

Nutty Egg Tart

1 tsp nutmeg
125 g chopped roasted hazelnuts
200 g honey
1 tbsp finely chopped fresh rosemary
4 tbsp sweet wine or sweet sherry
150 ml milk
2 eggs
Pastry to line a pie dish made with 225 g spelt flour and 100 g lard and water

Method

1. Make a dough from the spelt flour, lard and water. Line a pie dish and bake to make a pastry case.
2. Mix the chopped roasted hazelnuts with half the honey, rosemary and the sweet wine.
3. Spread this over a pre-baked pastry case.
4. Beat the eggs in the milk with the rest of the honey and pour over the nut mixture.
5. Sprinkle with nutmeg and bake in a moderate oven for 35 minutes or until firm and golden to touch.
6. Take out of the oven and sprinkle with more roasted chopped hazelnuts (these should sink slightly into the custard mixture).
7. Leave until cold before cutting. Serve on a platter decorated with rosemary leaves.

Honey Omelette

The Romans called this an 'egg sponge',
but it is clearly an omelette.

4 eggs

300 ml milk

125 g runny honey

3 tbsp olive oil

Cinnamon to taste

Method

1. Beat the eggs in the milk.
2. Heat the oil in a pan and then pour in the egg mixture.
3. Reduce the heat and cook until it is set.
4. Put onto a platter and pour the honey over the omelette when it is still hot.
5. Sprinkle with cinnamon and serve hot.

Sweet Toast

This is the Roman equivalent of French toast but without the egg. It is very simple, but very nice too!

Half a loaf of sliced bread with the crusts cut off

300 ml milk or enough to moisten the bread

3 tbsp olive oil

4 tbsp honey

Method

1. Soak the bread in the milk and drain excess off.
2. Heat the oil in the pan and, when hot, cook the bread in it until it is a golden colour.
3. Put onto a platter and drizzle with honey.
4. Eat with slices of fresh fruit.

A Dish of Spiced Pears

500 g hard pears
20 g honey
1 tbsp ground cumin
300 ml sweet wine
1 tsp olive oil
2 egg yolks

Method

1. Halve the pears and peel and core them.
2. Cover in water and poach until soft. Drain, keeping some of the liquid.
3. Into a pan, put 200ml of the pear liquid, wine, cinnamon, egg yolks and oil and heat gently until thickened.
4. Add pears to the pan and heat through. Serve at once.

A Dish of Spiced Peaches

500 g unripe peaches

1 tbsp cumin

1 tsp olive oil

1 tbsp honey

Method

1. Stone and cut the flesh into cubes and cover with water.
2. Simmer until tender.
3. Drain and sprinkle with oil, honey and cumin.
4. Serve cold and add more honey if it is not sweet enough.

Barley Drink

450 g pearl barley
1 litre sweet white wine
200 g honey
Water – enough to cover
barley when cooking

Method

1. Boil barley in water for 1 hour until cooked.
2. Drain, keeping liquid.
3. Mix in the wine with the barley water and sweeten to taste with honey.
4. Chill well before serving.

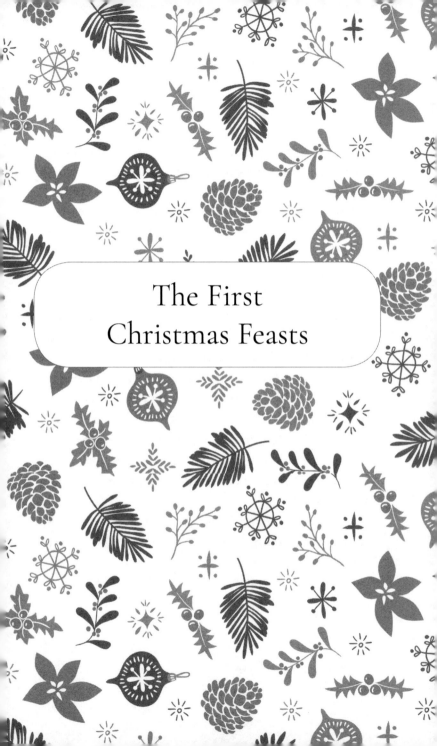

The First
Christmas Feasts

FOR THE FIRST three centuries after the Christian religion began it was outlawed by the Roman Empire, as we all know from our school text books. But what is little known is that the Romans were the first to celebrate the nativity on 25 December. The Emperor Constantine I became a Christian himself in AD 312 and from then on it became the official religion of the Roman Empire. Prior to this, the Romans had celebrated the Winter Solstice on 25 December. The earliest written record of the nativity being celebrated on this date was on an illuminated manuscript in Rome dated AD 354.

So the first lavish Christian nativity feasts would have been Roman. Apicius lived in the first century AD, but his cookbook was edited and republished in the fourth century AD, about the time of the first Christmas feasts. This is why Apicius's recipes were very likely to have been used during those original Christmas dinners.

So if you want to have a really original – in all senses of the word – Christmas dinner, why not try a Roman one!

Squash Alexandrine

1 medium-sized squash

½ tsp pepper

½ tsp cumin seeds

½ tsp coriander seeds

¼ cup chopped fennel bulb

2 tbsp chopped mint

2 tbsp cider vinegar

2 tbsp runny honey

150 ml boiled red wine

75 ml squash stock

2 tbsp olive oil

50 g chopped dates

50 g finely chopped walnuts

Method

1. Chop the squash flesh into cubes and boil until cooked.
2. Drain, saving the stock, and press out as much liquid as you can.
3. Sprinkle the cooked squash with salt and put in a pan.
4. Put the cumin, coriander, fennel, mint, nuts, dates, vinegar and honey in a blender or mortar and work until it is a paste.
5. Add this to the pan with the wine stock and olive oil and bring slowly to the boil. Simmer for 5 minutes.
6. Serve on a platter sprinkled with pepper and eat with chunks of bread.

Parsnips with Honey Sauce

6 large cooked parsnips

1 tbsp celery seeds

1 tsp finely chopped rosemary

2 tbsp runny honey

150 ml white wine

150 ml parsnip stock

1 tbsp olive oil

¼ tsp pepper

Flour to thicken

Method

1. Boil the sliced parsnips until tender and save the stock.
2. Mix celery seeds, rosemary, honey and pepper together in a pan with a little flour.
3. Add the other ingredients and bring to the boil, stirring until the sauce has thickened.
4. Pour over the parsnips and put in the oven to heat through for 10 minutes. Serve.

Nutty Scrambled Eggs

6 eggs

125 g pine nuts

125 g chopped hazelnuts

1 tbsp honey

¼ tsp pepper

1 tsp anchovy sauce

300 ml milk

1 tbsp olive oil

Anchovy fillets to decorate
the dish

Method

1. Toast the pine nuts and hazelnuts in the oil in a frying pan.
2. Beat the eggs with the milk and add the anchovy sauce, honey and pepper.
3. Add the egg mixture to the pan with the nuts, stirring constantly until the scrambled eggs are cooked.
4. Serve onto a platter and decorate with more pine nuts and anchovy fillets.

Cold Ham

2 kg ham

500 g dried figs

200 g runny honey

500 g spelt flour

150 ml olive oil

3 bay leaves

Method

1. Put the ham in water and bring to the boil. Boil for 30 minutes.
2. Discard the water and cover again with fresh water. Add the whole dried figs and the bay leaves.
3. Bring to the boil and simmer for 1 hour.
4. Drain, saving the figs, and, when cold, take off the skin of the ham.
5. Score the top into diamonds and drizzle the honey into the cracks.
6. Make a dough with the flour oil and water to mix.
7. Roll it out and cover the ham with it.
8. Bake for 30 minutes in a hot oven.
9. When cold, serve in slices with the crust on.

Apricot Relish for Ham

450 g whole fresh apricots
(underripe are best)

1 tsp cinnamon

1 tsp dried mint

3 tbsp honey

150 ml sweet muscatel wine

150 ml white wine

2 tbsp vinegar

2 tbsp olive oil

Pepper to taste

Method

1. Wash the apricots, stone them and put them in a pan in halves.
2. Mix cinnamon, mint, honey, vinegar and oil in a bowl.
3. Mix this with the wines and pour over the apricots.
4. Simmer gently for 1 hour, adding a little more wine if it becomes too dry.
5. When cold, arrange the whole apricots in a dish surrounded by the sauce.

Walnut and Fig Cakes

I made these for a TV programme and the camera crew ate them all as soon as we had finished filming, even though they all said they didn't usually eat very sweet food!

Dough

450 g spelt flour

200 ml olive oil

Water to mix

Filling

200 g walnuts

200 g dried figs

75 g honey

125 g olive oil

75 g runny honey
to serve with

Method

1. Mix the dough ingredients until pliable and leave to chill for 1 hour.
2. Chop the dates and walnuts finely and mix in the honey to make a paste.
3. Roll out the dough and cut into small rounds (use a wine glass as a cutter).
4. Place a teaspoon of the filling in the centre of each dough circle.
5. Moisten the edges and add another circle on top so you have little flying-saucer shapes.
6. Put the oil in a frying pan and, when hot, fry the pastries on both sides until golden brown.
7. Put onto a serving platter and drizzle with the rest of the honey. Serve hot or cold.

Dates Alexandrine

The cooking of these dates really changes the taste of them, as it caramelises the skin and is really delicious.

450 g whole dates

200 g whole blanched almonds

25 g cinnamon

125 g melted butter

200 g honey

Edible gold leaf to make them really special!

Method

1. Brush the almonds with butter and roll immediately in cinnamon.
2. Remove the stones of the dates, then stuff one almond into each cavity left behind.
3. Brush the date with warm honey.
4. Bake in a moderate oven for 5–10 minutes until the skin of the dates starts bubbling.
5. If you wish, you can place a strip of edible gold leaf on the dates for a festive look.
6. Lay them on a platter and serve with quarters of fresh figs or green grapes.

Spiced Wine Apicius

300 ml white wine

500 g honey

1 tsp pepper

½ tsp saffron

1 tsp cinnamon

4 dates, finely chopped

1 bay leaf

3½ quarts white wine

Method

1. Mix the wine with the honey in a pan and gently heat, stirring continuously.
2. Add the dates, pepper and saffron strands in a muslin bag with the bay leaf and powdered cinnamon.
3. Add the rest of the wine and heat gently. Simmer for 1 hour over a very low heat.
4. Take the spice bag out and serve either warm with a starter or hot with a dessert.

Basic conversion chart

Liquid, Volume

	Imperial	Metric
1/4tsp		1.2 ml
1/2 tsp		2.5 ml
1 tsp		5.0 ml
1/2 tbsp		7.5 ml
1 tbsp	1/2 fl oz	15 ml
1/8 cup	1 fl oz	30 ml
1/4 cup	2 fl oz	60 ml
1/3 cup	2 1/2 fl oz	80 ml
1/2 cup	4 fl oz	120 ml
2/3 cup	5 fl oz	160 ml
3/4 cup	6 fl oz	180 ml
1 cup	8 fl oz	250 ml

| Weight | | Temperature | |
Imperial	Metric	°F	°C
1/4 oz	7 g	200	90
1/2 oz	15 g	250	120
1 oz	30 g	300	150
2 oz	55 g	350	180
3 oz	85 g	400	200
4 oz (1/4 lb)	115 g	475	250
8 oz (1/2 lb)	225 g		
16 oz (1 lb)	250 g		

Bibliography

Andouze, F. & Buchsenschutz, O., *Towns, Villages and Countryside of Celtic Europe* (London: BCA, 1991)

Apicus, *The Roman Cookery of Apicius, translated and adapted by John Edwards* (London: Random House, 1984)

Armesto, Felipe Fernandez, *Food: A History* (London: Macmillan Ltd, 2001)

Berriedale-Johnson, Michelle, *The British Museum Cook Book* (London: British Museum Press, 1987)

Drummond, J.C. and Wilbraham, Anne, *The Englishman's Food* (London: Pimlico Ltd, 1939)

Dyer, J., *Ancient Britain* (Abingdon: Routledge, 1990)

Glasse, Hanna, *The Art of Cookery Made Easy*, facsimile edition by Karen Hess (Massachusetts: Applewood Books, 1997)

Mckendry, Maxime, *Seven Centuries of English Cooking* (London: C. Tinling & Co. Ltd, 1973)

Moss, Peter, *Meals Through The Ages* (London: George G. Harrap Ltd, 1958)

Parker Pearson, M., *Bronze Age Britain* (London: English Heritage, 1996)

Macready, S. & Thompson, F.H. *Cross-Channel Trade between Gaul and Britain in the Pre-Roman Iron Age* (London: Society of Antiquaries, 1984)

Piggot, S., *Ancient Europe* (Edinburgh: Edinburgh University Press, 1973)

Ross, A., *Everyday Life of the Pagan Celts* (London: Batsford, 1970)

Index

Also in the *Tasting the Past* series

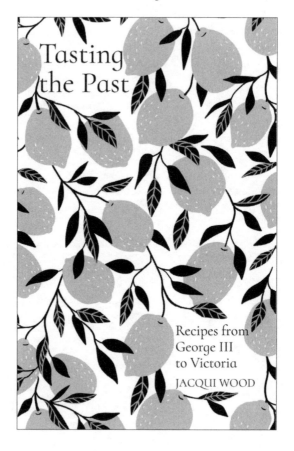

Tasting
the Past

Recipes from
George III
to Victoria

JACQUI WOOD

9780750992237

Also in this series

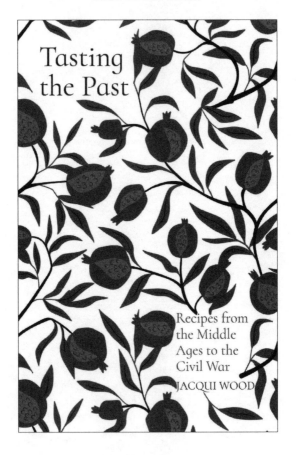

Tasting
the Past

Recipes from
the Middle
Ages to the
Civil War

JACQUI WOOD

9780750992244